BILL BELICHICK

JOHN FREDRIC EVANS

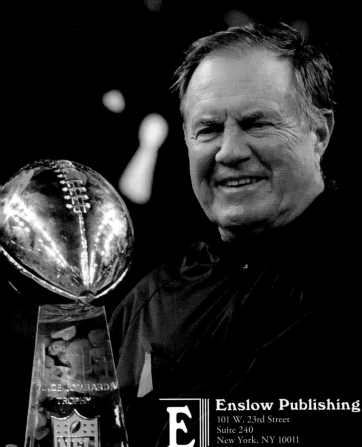

E

Enslow Publishing
101 W. 23rd Street
Suite 240
New York, NY 10011
USA

enslow.com

Published in 2020 by Enslow Publishing, LLC
101 W. 23rd Street, Suite 240, New York, NY 10011

Library of Congress Cataloging-in-Publication Data

Names: Evans, John Fredric, author.
Title: Bill Belichick / by John Fredric Evans. Description: New York : Enslow Publishing, 2020. | Series: Championship coaches | Includes bibliographical references and index. | Audience: Grade 7–12.
Identifiers: LCCN 2017055232| ISBN 9780766097940 (library bound) | ISBN 9780766097957 (pbk.)
Subjects: LCSH: Belichick, Bill—Juvenile literature. | Football coaches—United States—Biography—Juvenile literature. | New England Patriots (Football team)—Juvenile literature.
Classification: LCC GV939.B45 E83 2018 | DDC 796.332092 [B] —dc23
LC record available at https://lccn.loc.gov/2017055232

Printed in China

To Our Readers: We have done our best to make sure all website addresses in this book were active and appropriate when we went to press. However, the author and the publisher have no control over and assume no liability for the material available on those websites or on any websites they may link to. Any comments or suggestions can be sent by email to customerservice@enslow.com.

Photo Credits: Cover, pp. 1, 5, 16 Focus On Sport/Getty Images; p. 9 Tim Cammett/WireImage/Getty Images; p. 13 Paul Fearn/Alamy Stock Photo; pp. 20, 24, 33, 47, 75, 91 © AP Images; p. 26 Ronald C. Modra/Sports Imagery/Getty Images; p. 30 Sporting News Archive/Getty Images; p. 34 Bettmann/Getty Images; p. 39 Kirby Lee/Getty Images; p. 43 Al Bello/Getty Images; pp. 51, 87 Boston Globe/Getty Images; p. 55 Matt Campbell/AFP/Getty Images; p. 61 George Gojkovich/Getty Images; p. 66 Andy Lyons/Getty Images; p. 71 Nick Laham/Getty Images; p. 81 Jamie Squire/Getty Images; p. 92 Maddie Meyer/Getty Images.

CONTENTS

- - - - - - - - - - - - - - - -

INTRODUCTION

In the old days, National Football League teams could pretty much keep their players as long as they wanted. The future Hall of Famers drafted by the Steelers in the 1970s or the 49ers in the 1980s played their whole careers with the teams that took them, unless their employers decided to trade them away. Until a 1992 legal battle brought unrestricted free agency to the league, a championship team would probably bring back its best players, year after year.

In 2001–2002, Bill Belichick faced a very different landscape when he won his first Super Bowl as the head coach of the New England Patriots. Other teams watched the exploits of the Patriots along with the rest of the world, fully knowing that signing free agents from a Super Bowl winner would make a splash and sell tickets. The players' representatives knew this too and leveraged the success of their clients for bigger contracts. Even if a team wanted to pay the market rate for their players' services, they had to squeeze all contracts under a salary cap.

And yet Belichick has won more than 70 percent of his games with the Patriots, both in the regular season and the postseason. He has five Super Bowl rings. The team has done what the NFL tried to make

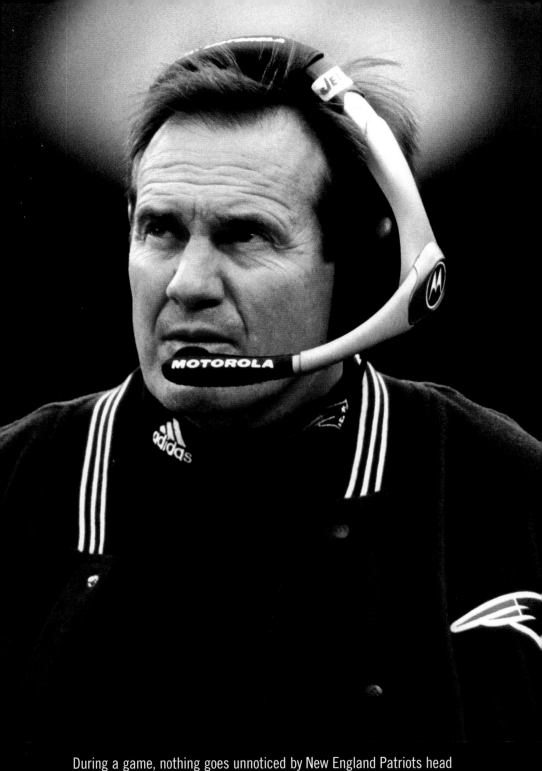

During a game, nothing goes unnoticed by New England Patriots head coach Bill Belichick, who has guided the team since 2000.

impossible, building a dynasty in an era when many forces try to tear the best teams apart. Belichick's old-fashioned team-first philosophy and perpetually evolving Xs and Os are a brilliant blend of adaptability and unwavering adherence to principle.

Belichick is widely acknowledged as one of the most flexible minds in the league, tailoring each week's game plan to the strengths and weaknesses of his opposition and even making strategic changes with a game in progress. He (along with his capable staff) is quick to pick up on the tiniest flaws in an opponent and capitalize upon them. No coach in the NFL makes more in-game adjustments than Belichick. He is also famous for scheming up defenses that take away an offense's best player, putting the ball in other, less-capable hands.

For all of his adaptability, there are rigid principles in Belichick's life and a decidedly "old-school" attitude about certain things. It's telling that in a society where selling yourself can seem integral to success in any walk of life, Bill Belichick doesn't believe in it. He sees self-marketing as, at best, empty posturing and worst, distracting self-indulgence. In Belichick's mind, the expression "all sizzle and no steak" applies to a lot of things. Belichick biographer David Halberstam wrote that he was "not only in the steak business, he had contempt for sizzle."

One thing that remains consistent is his advice to his players. Be prepared. Ignore the noise. Do your job. Intentionally mangling the names of social media platforms, Belichick shows disdain for "MyFace" and "Twittering" in his interactions with reporters. He makes a point of telling players to be wary, and preferably bland, when communicating in a public forum. Reporters will never goad Belichick into giving away too much at a "presser"—he comes to them thoroughly prepared for the specific questions he expects to hear.

Patriots owner Robert Kraft doesn't need his coach to be a showman. "One of the reasons I like him as a coach and human being is that he is never boastful and self-important," said Kraft. "He's not a phony, and to me, at this stage of my life, that's important. I'll say this: I've never known him to lie to me. He might not tell me something, but he's never told me a lie… I'm not saying he's always forthcoming."[1]

Love him or hate him, Bill Belichick is a legend of coaching for a reason. He approaches football with a rigor, focus, and clarity of purpose that would make him successful in any competitive endeavor.

1

BORN INTO A FOOTBALL FAMILY

In April 1952, Steve and Jeannette Belichick welcomed their only son into the world. Bill was born in Nashville, Tennessee, but the family soon moved to Annapolis, Maryland, where Steve coached at the US Naval Academy for thirty-four years. There, his most important task was to watch football and assess the performance of players in action. "He was always working. Every minute," Bill later said of his father. "He was like a hawk up there. And by watching him, I learned to see the game, how well prepared you have to be and how quickly your eyes have to shift."[1]

Bill's parents impressed on him the value of knowledge and integrity. His dad paid for the family home up front because he didn't

Steve Belichick, an assistant coach at Navy for thirty-four years, passed on his love of the game to his son Bill.

believe in borrowing or deferring payments, not even for a house. Bill's mother appreciated good writing so much that she kept dozens of copies of the *New Yorker* in the basement. There was no room for them upstairs, as hundreds of books already filled any available space.

HARD TIMES COME AGAIN

The misery of the Great Depression was still a vivid memory for Bill's parents and grandparents. Their stories of survival in extreme poverty stuck with Bill, even as he enjoyed a much more comfortable life as a child of the 1950s. He understood that hardship and sacrifice were often necessary to achieve success. But he also saw that doing what you love makes it a lot easier to work hard.

His father's story was instructive to Bill. Before beginning his freshman year of college with a football scholarship, an eighteen-year-old Steve Belichick toiled in a steel mill for five months. The sport rescued Steve from this punishing, low-paying work in the depths of the Depression. He was so grateful for the opportunity that he doubled as an assistant coach at the university later known as Case Western Reserve. Steve starred on the Navy football team, served during World War II, and then played in the National Football League. His love of the game only grew stronger, and in fact it was contagious.

Bill saw that his dad came home from work happy and was eager to go back in the morning. While other kids collected postage stamps or baseball cards, Bill preferred to study football film with Dad. He soon discovered that film gives you an edge, as a player or a coach. Where players lined up, the quarterback's different intonations for running plays and passing plays—these were all clues telling a perceptive "film grinder" how to defeat that team.

Bill came to realize that finding an opponent's weaknesses wasn't the key. Figuring out how to take away what they did best and neutralize their strength was how you won.

At nine years old, Bill was given his own copy of Navy's game plan every week—assuming he'd finished his homework, that is. His dad often brought him to work with him, said Phil Savage, an assistant with Belichick in Cleveland. "Bill would end up in a room or a closet by himself with a projector and a stack of film, and it's like, 'Son, take these tapes and tell me how many times they ran split back.' And Bill just devoured it. He always saw video and film and the mental side of the game as the great equalizer for him."[2]

During practices Bill caught passes from Roger Staubach, a

The Navy's Sharp-Eyed Scout

Bill's father, Steve, had twenty/fifteen eyesight and keen peripheral vision, which made him a natural scout because he could easily track the many moving parts in a football play. He became known for seeing the subtle giveaways that reveal what opponents will do before they do it, an edge that helped the US Naval Academy get to more bowl games in his thirty-four-year career than with any other coach in school history. His 1962 book, *Football Scouting Methods*, is considered a must-read for young coaches.

star at Navy in the early 1960s who went on to win two Super Bowls as the quarterback of the Dallas Cowboys. "Being around the Naval Academy, of course, is a very unique atmosphere, particularly as it relates to football," said Belichick. "The teamwork that comes with that and the commitment that those players have, I saw at a young age."[3]

By the time he entered high school, Bill knew he wasn't a gifted athlete—he had what scouts call "slow feet." Still, he loved the game so much he went out for football anyway. Bill learned a great deal from Al Laramore, his coach at Annapolis High. There were no names on the school's jerseys. Kids only played in the fall if they earned it through many grueling hours of practice in the summer, and starters were usually seniors. For

> "I wasn't aware of it at the time, but I can see how that molded me."[4]
>
> —Bill Belichick

Laramore, commitment was more important than talent. The team played a hard-nosed brand of power football, generally running the same four plays (only one of them a passing play) over and over. The other team always knew they were coming, but Laramore's boys were so tough and well conditioned that the plays were still hard to stop.

Bill knew so much even then that for the team it was like having an assistant coach on the field. He volunteered insights and suggestions to the coaches privately.

MENTOR IN MASSACHUSETTS

To be certain he got into a good college, Bill enrolled at Andover Prep, a prestigious boarding school in Massachusetts. He found it academically demanding and struggled at first but soon adopted the study habits necessary to excel. Steve Sorota, head coach of the football team, had lessons to impart, as well. Sorota possessed the same "eye of the hurricane" calm Bill maintains during stressful moments in big games. Sorota's calm steadied his players in turbulent times, and it's no accident that someone who knew both men called Belichick a "partial reincarnation" of the Andover coach.[5]

That someone was Ernie Adams, who met Bill in their senior year at Andover. Forming a lifelong friendship, they would coach together with the New York Giants, Cleveland Browns, and New

As a student at Andover Prep, Bill Belichick admired his coach and found a friend with whom to unravel football's mysteries.

England Patriots. Every bit as brainy as Bill, Ernie bought Steve Belichick's book at age fourteen and that's why he sought out Steve's son at school. Growing up, these kindred spirits had both been caught with football plays diagrammed in school notebooks. Now they snuck into Boston College practices to "scout." They were also teammates on an undefeated Andover squad coached by Sorota. It's no surprise the duo would spend decades working together to unravel the game's deepest mysteries.

Bill's performance at Andover got him into Wesleyan University, where his main takeaway was that there was also a *wrong* way to do things. Blindsided in practice with an ethically borderline chop block that broke his leg, Belichick was dismayed that such tactics were used at all, let alone practiced on one's own teammates. At Andover,

> "Ernie's very, very smart. He has great historical perspective. Sometimes that comes into play."[6]
>
> —Bill Belichick

Sorota's practices went out of their way to avoid injury, keeping hitting to a minimum and teaching players that proper use of leverage was more important than raw power.

After graduating, Belichick had no obvious path into the coaching profession. He sent out more than 250 inquiry letters. His dad's shining reputation could open doors for Belichick, but he was still a mediocre player from small-time programs. Football coaches look out for each other, however, at every level of the sport. Every victory was also a defeat for those on the other team, and coaches knew the circumstances could be reversed the next week or the next season. An athletic director, owner, or coach could replace assistants at will, prompting a frantic job search that might force families to uproot and move cross-country. The colleague you helped today might help you tomorrow.

And so, through a tangled web of relationships and intercon-nected coaches that traced back to his father's career, Belichick landed his first gig in the National Football League.

A Pigskin Prodigy

Ernie Adams has always been ahead of the curve. Before he left junior high he wasn't playing on the intramural football team, he was coaching it. At seventeen, he was booted from the Boston University bleachers for taking scouting notes on an intra-squad game, though he didn't yet work for any team. But Adams was also a scholarship student and the best Latin scholar at Andover, where he met Bill Belichick. Adams attended Northwestern because it had the top Latin pro-gram in the nation, and he wowed his way onto the coaching staff with his photographic memory.

In 1975, Baltimore Colts coach Ted Marchibroda showed a young Belichick how things were done at the highest level of football.

2

STUDENT OF THE GAME

- - - - - - - - - - - - - - -

Belichick had several connections to the Baltimore Colts, most through his father. The Colts' new head coach, Ted Marchibroda, heeded the recommendation of one of Steve's colleagues and brought on Bill in an unpaid position. Far from their glory days of the 1950s with Johnny Unitas at quarterback, the penny-pinching Colts were not keen on paying an unproven assistant coach, especially one who was younger than many of their players. Bill was twenty-two at the time. Years later Steve Belichick said to Bill's biographer, David Halberstam, "I think that Ted was thinking the kid could come up and break down film for him and maybe get four tickets per game."[1]

Though he was initially a gofer, the team soon saw that Belichick was a natural at "grinding film." At the pro level most teams are roughly equal athletically. Unlocking the secrets found on game film is the best way to gain an edge, but few coaches want to put in the time required to do so. Belichick couldn't get enough. He slept in the office, working around the clock. Sometimes he would find something on the film at 3 a.m. and wake up the Colts' defensive coordinator with an idea for the week's game plan. Belichick was always willing to do the grunt work others weren't willing to do and, at least at first, he did it for free.

In Baltimore, Bill was not that well liked, especially by offensive players. They called him nicknames like "the Punk," "the Turk," and "Bad News Bill." There is a degree of machismo in every football player, and some chose to test the authority of the young physically unimposing coach. Even then Belichick would not be intimidated and didn't care how popular he was among the players.

From Friends to Rivals

While a coaching intern with the Baltimore Colts, Belichick met sixteen-year-old Jim Irsay, whose father, Robert, owned the team. Jim was lending a hand in the equipment room, picking up towels and jock straps. "Bill clearly contributed that season," Irsay said. "He helped in whatever area Ted [Marchibroda] needed him." Irsay took over in 1997, and his team, by then in Indianapolis, became one of the Patriots' fiercest playoff rivals during Belichick's tenure. "His mental toughness, his ability to stay in this league, compete year after year and produce outstanding teams, is remarkable,"[2] said Irsay in 2015.

BALTIMORE TAKES NOTICE

They began taking Belichick seriously when they noticed that, week after week, no one knew more about the opposing team. The information he gave players helped them do their jobs better. Baltimore ran an attacking defense based on scouting opponents' tendencies in film study. The key to their scheme was to seize the initiative rather than be reactive. To do this a defense must know what the offense plans to do in many different situations. Defenders can't wait to see what happens after the ball is snapped.

Belichick was a natural at picking up a player's "tells," small, unconscious tip-offs like positioning his feet differently when the play call was a run. If the defense knew what was coming, they could *act* rather than *react*. Belichick's film study helped him prepare the team, and the defense improved game to game.

> *"I wouldn't be here if not for Ted Marchibroda...I learned so much from him."*[3]
>
> —Bill Belichick

Bill went from unpaid intern to receiving $25 a week to joining the defensive coaching staff, all before the end of the preseason. By midseason his pay had doubled. Marchibroda was impressed by the way Belichick attacked any assignment, from bed check for players and breaking down film to grabbing takeout lunch. At the end of a successful 10–4 campaign the coach desperately wanted to give Belichick the modest raise necessary to keep him, even then at a

In his four-year apprenticeship, Belichick learned the intricacies of offense, defense, and special teams.

"hometown discount," but the penny-pinching general manager refused. Belichick took a vastly better offer on the table.

Belichick was sad to leave that coaching staff, however. Later he said he learned a lot more from Marchibroda than Xs and Os. "It was a lot more about just being a football coach, being a professional, preparation, work ethic, dependability, what goes into having a good football team."[4]

HAVE WHISTLE, WILL TRAVEL

Working as special teams assistant and receivers coach for the Detroit Lions, Belichick again distinguished himself with tireless dedication. "I think a lot of it came from the fact that he had not played big-time football, and because of that he felt he had to work twice as hard as anyone else, to prove himself,"[5] said Floyd Reese, also an assistant on the staff. It started when Belichick aced a playbook pop quiz given to all coaching candidates. Reese wondered if, with a mind like that, Belichick would soon leave the game and become the CEO of some Fortune 500 company.

Belichick approached each staff meeting as though it were a master's class in coaching. He didn't say much at first but sponged up all the football talk, watched how other coaches worked, and took note of what he liked. Though Belichick's professional focus was defense, he knew he had to understand how offensive coaches thought. In Detroit he learned the other side of the ball from one of the best minds of the era, in his opinion. Coordinator Ken Shipp ran sophisticated offenses that read defense very quickly.

Family Business

In high school, Bill met his future wife, Debby Clarke, and they married in 1977. In 1993, the couple founded a charity organization to raise money for the homeless and needy in Cleveland and Massachusetts. They have three children: Amanda, Stephen, and Brian. Stephen is the Patriots' safeties coach, while Brian joined the team as a scouting assistant in 2016. Amanda is the head coach of the lacrosse team at College of the Holy Cross in Massachusetts. Bill and Debby divorced in 2006.

With the Denver Broncos, in the final stop of his apprenticeship tour, Belichick learned from a former Oakland coach about Raiders owner Al Davis's practice of constant evaluation, assessing the performance of players (and coaches) on a continual basis. He also appreciated that the Broncos'

"Talent sets the floor, character sets the ceiling."[6]

—**Bill Belichick**

defense featured unheralded but essential players who understood and appreciated the importance of their roles. All of these ideas would become hallmarks of a Belichick team.

Leaving Denver in 1979, Belichick knew the future looked bright. He'd had a great learning experience in the course of four years in three cities, working with wonderful teachers, and would borrow a piece here and a piece there when building teams of his own. His varied responsibilities with each franchise had broadened and deepened his understanding of the game, in all aspects. "By the time I got through those four years, I felt I had been around the block on a lot of different levels," said Belichick. "I had seen a lot of different players and head-coaching styles."[7]

He was ready to make a name for himself in his area of specialty: defense.

3

A GIANT LEAP

- - - - - - - - - - - - - - - -

Naturally, it was Ernie Adams who got Belichick his first big
break. As a member of the Patriots organization, Adams worked
with assistant coach Ray Perkins for two years. The staff was amazed
by Adams's ability to memorize a playbook and recall anything he
saw on film. When Perkins became the head coach of the New York
Giants, he hired Adams as his quarterbacks coach. Adams recom-
mended his friend Belichick, of course, so in 1979 the twenty-seven-
year-old joined the "G-Men" as a defensive assistant.

The Giants were coming off several middling seasons. The team
culture needed an overhaul, and Perkins was the man to do it. He
ran long, hard practices that instilled toughness and discipline in
his players. By the time Perkins handed the reins to Bill Parcells and
took his dream job at his alma mater, Alabama, the Giants were on
their way back to respectability.

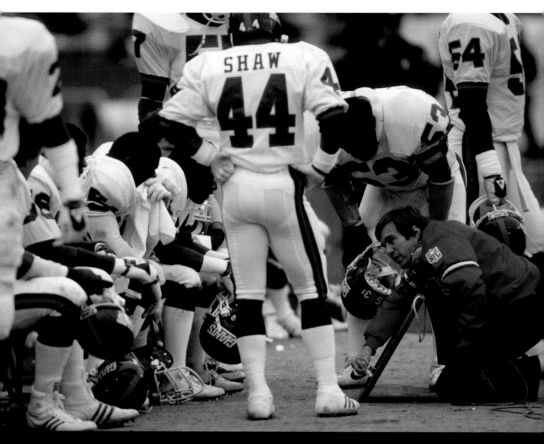

As the defensive coordinator of the New York Giants, Belichick quickly distinguished himself as one of the best young minds in the game.

TWO BILLS ARE BETTER THAN ONE?

Though their partnership would become famously successful, the same first name was about the only thing Parcells and Belichick had in common. Parcells was a big man, while Belichick was not. Parcells's coaching tool of choice was emotion, and Belichick's was strategy. Parcells was less an Xs and Os man than a master motivator, and his players would do anything to avoid being branded "soft" or ridiculed by their sardonic coach.

While Parcells was a master of fanning the flames in a player's heart, Belichick knew that he didn't have that gift. His method was to give players a leg up so they'd perform better—his insights into the opposition made his players more confident and purposeful, so they listened to him and did what he told them to do. Every good play, good game, and good season brought them closer to their ultimate goal—to make a lot of money in the few years the typical professional football player has to do so.

By the mid-1980s the Giants were a fearsome team, and the synergy between Parcells and Belichick brought out the best in both of them. Belichick was the yin to Parcells's yang. They agreed on what kind of football they wanted to play—a grind-it-out offense takes time off the

The Turnaround Artist

Bill Parcells is famous for taking over a team in the doldrums and rapidly getting it back on track. He is the only coach to lead four different teams to the NFL playoffs, taking three of them to the conference championship game. Each team he took over had won five or fewer games the previous season. And all four times Parcells had the team in the postseason by his second season. Most impressively, he took over a 1–15 Jets team and completed the best two-year turnaround in NFL history, going 9–7 and 12–4 with an AFC Championship Game appearance.

clock, allowing a physical, punishing defense to rest and reenter the game in a favorable situation. That defense focused on stopping the run first and foremost.

Belichick became the defensive coordinator, and his creative schemes were admired by opponents and the media alike. Considered Parcells's top lieutenant, the man nicknamed "Doom and Gloom" and "Little Bill" gained a reputation as someone who tormented opposing quarterbacks with the confusing looks his defenses gave them.

With that in mind, the team drafted for defense and equipped Belichick with a world-class group of linebackers. Pacing the pack was Lawrence Taylor. Uncannily strong for 250 pounds (113 kilograms),

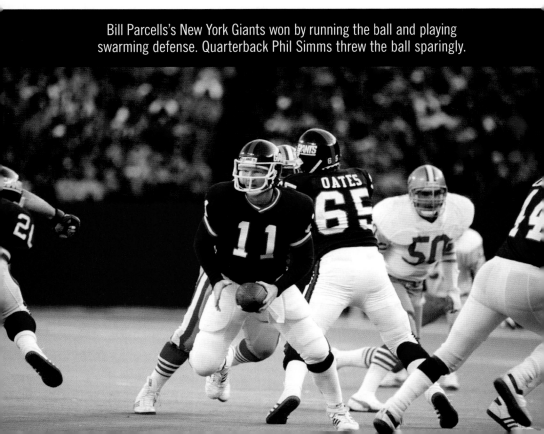

Bill Parcells's New York Giants won by running the ball and playing swarming defense. Quarterback Phil Simms threw the ball sparingly.

Taylor moved like a great white shark and hit with the force of a rhinoceros. Taylor could fend off a blocker with one hand while figuring out where to be next and almost instantly get there when he decided. What's more, he always knew what every other player on the defense should be doing. He recognized the pivotal plays that decided games and always found his highest gear in those moments, rising to the occasion.

Like his father before him, Belichick was excited to go to work every morning. With such talent at his disposal, Belichick could achieve greatness if he prepared his players well enough. The competition in the NFC was fierce, to the point that reaching the conference championship game was a tremendous achievement. After the Los Angeles Raiders' Super Bowl win in 1983, the next AFC squad to hoist the Lombardi Trophy was the Denver Broncos in 1998.

> *[Lawrence Taylor was] the best defensive player I've ever coached, by a good margin."* [1]
>
> —Bill Belichick

At the end of the 1986 season, the Giants played the Washington Redskins for the right to face the Denver Broncos in the Super Bowl. Washington was almost unbeatable if they had the lead in the second half, but the defense known as the Big Blue Wrecking Crew shut down their running game and cruised to a 17–0 halftime lead. Forced to throw in the second half, the Redskins passed on thirty-four of thirty-seven plays and lost this one-sided game.

Belichick's first Super Bowl presented a formidable challenge in Denver quarterback John Elway, a magician in the pocket who often left defenders grasping for air before he launched a perfectly accurate spiral to a receiver given time to break open against any defender. Belichick knew that containing Elway was the key. The Giants were able to do that, and New York's dialed-in Phil Simms completed a record twenty-two of his twenty-five passes. The Giants won the Super Bowl by a 39–20 score, giving Belichick the first of his seven championship rings.

"WIDE RIGHT"

The NFC's dominance continued, and it was another four years before the Giants made it back to the big game, despite fielding powerful teams every season. To get there in 1990–1991 they had to defeat Joe Montana's San Francisco 49ers on a field goal with four seconds left on the clock. That year Belichick's defense faced the Hall-of-Fame quarterback twice and held him to 23 total points, denying the Niners their third straight trip to the Super Bowl.

Instead it was the Giants who would face the seemingly unstoppable Buffalo Bills in the 1991 Super Bowl, which is still regarded as one of the most exciting ever played. The league's number-one offense faced the number-one defense. Buffalo had the stars to offset

> *"We're going to let Thurman Thomas get 100 yards."*[2]
>
> —Bill Belichick

Belichick's studly linebackers. Their dynamic passing attack featured quarterback Jim Kelly and wide receivers James Lofton and Andre Reed. All three were voted into the Hall of Fame once their playing days were done.

Buffalo's offensive coordinator was Belichick's mentor, Ted Marchibroda, who had before instituted a new wrinkle that would soon become a staple of offenses. The no-huddle brought to every play the same fast pace that most teams employed only in the last two minutes of a half or game. It exhausted defenses and allowed little time to adjust to how the offense lined up.

Belichick decided on a bold

Pepper Patrolled the Middle

Thomas "Pepper" Johnson got his nickname when his aunt noticed him putting pepper on his cereal. The Giants drafted the linebacker in the second round of the 1986 NFL Draft, and he played for Bill Belichick on both of New York's Super Bowl champion teams. In 1993, Johnson joined Belichick with the Browns. He also played the final two seasons of his career with Belichick, as a member of the Jets. Johnson then coached linebackers and linemen for the Patriots from 2000 to 2014. Belichick spent more years working with Johnson than any other player or coach.

strategy that ran counter to everything the Giants stood for. Every week their goal was to permit the other team's star running back no more than 90 yards rushing. But now, about to play on the world's biggest stage, Belichick told the defense that if they allowed Buffalo running back Thurman Thomas to rush for at least 100, they would

Bill Belichick's defensive game plan for the 1991 Super Bowl was so effective that it was enshrined in the Pro Football Hall of Fame.

win the game.[3] Buffalo's offense could do the most damage through the air, and the Giants' game plan was to control the clock, limiting Jim Kelly's opportunities to gobble up yards and score points in a hurry. If it looked as though the running game was working, the Bills might opt for the more time-consuming carries and gain smaller chunks of yardage.

"I think the running game was the least of our concerns in that game," Belichick said. "I always felt when we needed to stop the run, we could stop it. And the more times they ran it, it was just one less time they could get it to Reed or get it to Lofton, or throw it to Thomas, who I thought was more dangerous as a receiver, because there's more space than there was when he was a runner."[4]

Belichick's players were incredulous at first, but they believed in him. The Giants led 12–10 at halftime, a good place to be against a team that had blown away its last two opponents by a combined score of 95 to 37. In the second half, New York's clock-devouring drives kept the Bills' high-powered offense off the field. Buffalo owned the ball for a mere 19:27 of the game's 60 minutes. Still, with four seconds left Buffalo had a chance to win the game with a long field goal. Kicker Scott Norwood's boot was famously "wide right" and New York hung on, winning 20–19. It remains the only Super Bowl decided by a single point.

True to Belichick's prediction, Thurman Thomas had 135 yards rushing. Belichick's defensive game plan was enshrined in the Pro Football Hall of Fame.

Belichick was typically modest in assessing why his team won. "I think games are won by players," Belichick said. "The coach tries to put the players in a position where they have a chance to compete, but players are the ones that make the plays…[You can] put anything you want down on a piece of paper, but you've got to have players to go out there and play, and we had that."[5]

4

BROKEN-HEARTED BROWNS

Fresh off his second Super Bowl as the Giants' defensive coordinator, Belichick was a hot commodity. The next logical step was his first head-coaching job, and the offers came rolling in.

HEADING TO OHIO

He went with Cleveland, a team that had been on the brink of a Super Bowl appearance three out of the previous four years. In fact, the 1986 Browns suffered an improbable AFC Championship loss to the same Denver team Belichick's defense throttled in the Super Bowl a week later. Adding to the franchise's appeal was its impressive

After winning their second Super Bowl together, it was time for Belichick and Parcells to part ways.

history dating back to the 1940s. A student of the game, Belichick admired former Browns coach Paul Brown (from whom the team took its name) and the countless innovations he brought to the sport. Finally, the team's passionate fans packed the stadium in good times and bad.

"I'm not running for mayor of Cleveland."[1]

—Bill Belichick

As the head coach of the Cleveland Browns, Belichick realized that
his Xs and Os were sound but his people skills needed work.

For Belichick though, it wasn't meant to be in Cleveland. He butted
heads with Browns owner Art Modell, who was his philosophical
opposite. Where Belichick was about doing, Modell was about selling. A PR man from New York, he didn't have the deep pockets of
other NFL owners and set lofty expectations for the team, hoping to
boost season ticket sales. This despite the fact Cleveland was 3–13
the year before Belichick arrived. Modell wanted him to sell the team

to the media, but Belichick had never faced microphones before—in New York, Parcells's assistant coaches were forbidden from talking to the press. Not that Belichick had any interest in holding court from the podium, anyway.

Modell had granted the media great access to the team, which Belichick, following Parcells's lead, immediately stripped away. This did not endear him to the press. "I clamped down on them," Belichick said. "It could have been done in a more positive or gracious way...I take responsibility for it. But the bottom line was we just didn't win quickly enough."[2] Indeed, Cleveland was 6–10 and 7–9 (twice) in Bill's first three seasons with the team.

As the youngest coach in the league by a full six years, Belichick overcompensated by being extremely hard on his players. He cursed them out for small mistakes and maintained an authoritarian, impersonal distance. Without question, Belichick's people skills were lacking at that stage of his career. A caller into his radio show wished

Cleveland Rocks?

It is a little-known fact that Bill Belichick is a "closet rock 'n' roll nut,"[3] in the words of former Cleveland Browns assistant Rick Venturi. Belichick and Browns defensive coordinator Nick Saban shared a stress reliever. "He and I used to sneak out and go see various concerts," Saban remembered. "We went to see the Eagles, Joe Walsh, Ringo Starr."[4] Belichick once invited his whole coaching staff to a Pink Floyd concert. Jon Bon Jovi, to this day a Belichick favorite and friend, was a regular at Browns practices.

him a Merry Christmas and the response was twenty seconds of dead air. He once muttered, "I don't give a [darn] what the fans think" into an open microphone.

What wasn't widely known was that after big wins Belichick walked around the building and dropped hundred-dollar bills on the desks of coaches, scouts, and administrative assistants, just to thank them for the work they did. "It was the kind of gesture people would never, ever connect to Bill Belichick," said Phil Savage, a Browns assistant during the Belichick regime. "There's a generosity to Bill most people don't get to see."[5]

Despite the owner's high expectations, when Belichick looked at the team he saw an over-the-hill group with few young bucks on the way up. Compared to the physically and mentally tough Giants, this team was Charmin soft. Belichick's public statements were guarded, even pessimistic, leading one of the Browns' top beat writers to call him "the voice of doom."

The Browns star whose deterioration was most alarming to Belichick was quarterback Bernie Kosar. A folk hero in Cleveland and engineer of those playoff runs that fell just short, Kosar was above criticism in the eyes of the fans, and the media. But Belichick— and defensive coordinators around the league—saw what they didn't. Over the years, Kosar's body had taken a beating playing behind inferior offensive lines. Never mobile, the aging quarterback was now ponderous in the pocket, and the strength in a so-so arm had waned to the point that Kosar made excuses for not testing it with difficult throws. This infuriated Belichick, who could not operate the offense he wanted with Kosar at the controls.

Things came to a head when Kosar threw a touchdown pass in a game and told the media afterward that he had drawn up the play in the dirt, a veiled shot at his head coach. The next day Belichick announced that Kosar had been released, citing his "diminished skills" in a cold-blooded press conference. For the city this was a favorite son being exiled by an unpopular outsider. Belichick would later express regret for his handling of the Kosar affair, which had left the Cleveland faithful little room to appreciate his perspective. The fans would not forgive, even a year later when the team hosted a home playoff game.

By then Belichick and Saban had built a great defense, with the 1994 team surrendering the fewest points in the league that year and qualifying for the playoffs with an 11–5 record. In the wild card round, the Browns defeated a Patriots team coached by Bill Parcells. They were ousted by the Steelers a week later.

Though he had only the one winning season in Cleveland, it can't be said that Belichick didn't work hard enough. And he expected his staff to share his commitment. "[Nick] Saban might be the greatest college coach ever, and I can honestly say in the last eight years at Alabama I have never once seen him tired," said Phil Savage. "But in Cleveland, under Bill, he'd go slump down against a wall and stutter, 'I gotta' get out of here, I can't function anymore.' Bill could outwork all of us."[6]

The next year, Modell suddenly decided to move the team to Baltimore. "Once they announced the move, 1995 became as bad as anything I've ever been through from a football standpoint," said Rick Venturi, then the Browns' offensive coordinator. "A total, miserable death slide. It went from the greatest sports city in the world to an 80,000-person wake on Sundays. Bill would never show it, but it took a toll on him."[7]

The Browns' name and history would remain in Cleveland. A few months later, Belichick was fired and his old boss, Ted Marchibroda, was hired to coach the Baltimore Ravens in their first year of existence. What to do next would soon seem obvious.

PATRIOTIC DUTY

While Belichick was in Cleveland, Parcells had moved on to New England. The franchise had been mostly hapless throughout its history. The only time the Patriots made it to the Super Bowl, they were crushed by the Chicago Bears, 46–10. On the rare occasions they were good, the team suffered misfortunes such as dubious officiating (in a 1976 playoff loss to the Raiders), their head coach taking another job on the eve of the playoffs (Chuck Fairbanks, in 1978) and high-profile distractions (a 1985 drug scandal).

Parcells took over a team that posted a 9–39 record over the previous three seasons. It was a roller-coaster ride at first, with a playoff appearance (the loss to Belichick's Browns) being followed by a 6–10 season that demanded changes be made. Belichick was now available, and a reunion of "the Bills" made sense for everyone. After all, they'd worked together for eight successful years with the Giants. Belichick became the Pats' defensive coordinator.

New owner Robert Kraft didn't want to give total personnel control to Parcells, who'd been hired by the prior regime. The ever-colorful "Big Tuna" chafed under Kraft's oversight, and Belichick served as a referee of sorts between coach and owner. "Obviously a lot of things

From Fan to Owner

Born in Boston, Robert Kraft grew up rooting for the Patriots. As a young father, he bought season tickets for his family before they could afford it. His dream was to bring a championship to Foxboro, and he spent years trying to buy the team. In fact, he owned their stadium long before purchasing the franchise in 1994. "I think people have always, throughout his life, underestimated him," Jonathan Kraft said of his father. "He didn't come from a lot financially...He would be told he didn't have the resources, or the smarts, or whatever it was...But he'd be tenacious and stick with it."[8]

In Bill Belichick, Bob Kraft chose the right coach to make his championship dreams come true. But he also empowered Belichick to make his own decisions.

had happened before I had gotten there," said Belichick. "My sense of it was there wasn't a lot of communication."[9] There was often communication between Belichick and Kraft, with Belichick mentoring Kraft on football and Kraft sharing his business acumen.

The Parcells Patriots made it to the Super Bowl but lost to Brett Favre and the Green Bay Packers. The conflict over personnel decisions ended with Parcells's departure to the New York Jets with the famous quote, "If they want you to cook the dinner, at least they can let you shop for some of the groceries."[10]

Though Belichick went with Parcells to New York, their relationship gradually eroded with the Jets. Parcells's "guys" clashed with Belichick's own loyal disciples. Then, after three mostly successful seasons, the Jets lost their owner and the team was put up for sale.

Parcells stepped down but would serve as general manager. He offered the job to Belichick, who was leery of the unsettled ownership situation. What if the new owner brought in a general manager whose team-building philosophy clashed with his?

> *"I resigned because I wasn't comfortable with the situation with the Jets."*[11]
>
> **—Bill Belichick**

By rejecting the Jets job in the press conference arranged to announce his acceptance, Belichick made it clear that he was Parcells's second-in-command no longer. This made for yet another awkward, rambling media appearance in a career with no shortage of them.

While Kraft wanted Belichick to lead his team in 2000, Belichick was still technically under contract with the Jets. Parcells reached out to Kraft to hammer out a deal. "I told him it was Darth Vader calling, and he said he knew who that was,"[12] Parcells said. After sharing a laugh and mending fences, Kraft agreed to send New York a first-round draft pick as compensation for releasing Belichick from his contract.

It was in this unorthodox fashion that Bill Belichick became the head coach of the New England Patriots. "Hopefully, this press conference will go a little better than the last one I had," Belichick said, referring to the clumsy monologue he delivered when he resigned in New York. When asked if he left the Jets to escape Parcells's legacy, he said, "If I wanted to get out of Bill's shadow, I wouldn't have come to New England. There's a shadow up here, too."[13]

5

A NEW WAY TO WIN

- - - - - - - - - - - - - -

One of the things Kraft and Belichick had always seen eye to eye on was the concept of player value in the salary cap era. Teams had to ensure that their combined player contracts did not exceed a given number, which increased slightly every year. With the cap, balanced scheduling, and the impact success had on the market for a free agent's services, it seemed impossible to maintain that success over an extended period of time.

In New England, coach and owner agreed that the right model was to assemble a team of modestly paid players who complemented each other. They wanted as many roughly interchangeable players as possible, believing that a deep roster could maintain its level of play despite losing players to decline, injuries, or free agency. It would also be a long-term plan, not a "win now" scheme.

Players like Troy Brown fit the Belichick mold
perfectly: versatile, tough-minded, and professional.

Another reason Belichick and Kraft got along so well was that
Belichick didn't need absolute control over personnel matters. He
knew he couldn't coach a team and keep up with pro and college
scouting, so he saw the value in having a general manager. Belichick
quickly reached out to his old friend Scott Pioli, who came on as the
Pats' VP of player personnel.

EYE TO THE FUTURE

Pioli and Belichick instituted a firm but flexible scouting system. Its grading scale was easy to understand but detailed enough to reflect, for example, the value of an average offensive lineman who could play two positions on the line versus an above-average lineman who could play one only. The team they wanted would be bigger, stronger, and faster than most; tough enough to practice and play in the unpredictable weather of the Northeast; and infused with both passion and football smarts.

At the beginning of Belichick's first season, the team was already over the salary cap. As they could not target the top-tier free agents, Belichick and Pioli sought out the best stopgap players. They turned first to Belichick's former players from the Giants and Jets, guys who knew his system and trusted his methods. Still, Belichick believed that in the salary cap era it would be unwise to reward someone for past contributions. The value of any contract must be based on what a player could

An Old Friend

Bill and Scott Pioli go back to summer 1986, when Belichick was a Giants assistant and Pioli a college student visiting Giants camp to watch the team practice. When a mutual friend introduced them they hit it off immediately. Belichick even let Pioli sleep on his couch. Later, in Cleveland, Belichick hired Pioli as a scouting assistant. Though Pioli stayed with the franchise through its move to Baltimore, he rejoined Belichick as the Jets' pro personnel director when Belichick ran the defense. Belichick's boss of eight years, Bill Parcells, is Pioli's father-in-law.

contribute in the future. This belief would inform Belichick's decisions for years to come, giving him a justified reputation as an unsen-
timental leader.

Belichick knew the team was more than a few pieces away from
being a championship contender, but he still felt the pressure to win
or forever be relegated to second-banana status. Now forty-seven,
he knew he might not get
another head-coaching gig if
he couldn't make it work in
New England. He was going
to give this all he had, and he
expected his players to do the

> *"It's not about collecting talent, it's about assembling a team."*[1]
> —Bill Belichick

same. "Bill came into that first training camp and you could see his
plan being executed," said Damien Woody, a second-year center in
2000. "He was on top of everyone. It didn't matter who you were, he
was coaching you up hard. I had played the year before, but I felt like
I was seeing a different NFL. I knew it was going to be tough."[2]

The 2000 Patriots were a vanilla bunch, just good enough to lose
their first four games by a combined twenty-one points en route to a
5–11 record. Still, Belichick's defense kept them in games, even without star players. In the fourth quarter of most games, the team was
still within striking distance on the scoreboard. In a Bill Belichick
defense, every player can potentially blitz and every player can potentially drop into coverage. This confuses quarterbacks. Meanwhile,
the defense funnels ball carriers to smart linebackers who are good

tacklers, preventing big gains for the offense. In 2000, the system was already working, even if the talent was nothing to rave about.

PUTTING THE PIECES IN PLACE

The next off-season would set the table for the Patriots' shocking run to the Super Bowl. The front office added players who weren't seen as big-ticket talents but fit the system perfectly. One such player was Mike Vrabel, an undersized defensive end in college whose first team tried to bulk up because they were loaded at line-backer. It didn't work. Still, the versatile Vrabel was perfect for the Patriots' scheme and made a number of memorable plays over the next few seasons.

The 2001 draft yielded defensive lineman Richard Seymour, whom New England drafted despite a more obvious need at receiver. The pick was widely panned by reporters. Mature beyond his years, Seymour could play multiple positions and his intangibles were off the charts. He would be a key contributor for years to come. And still tucked away

> *"The strength of the wolf is the pack."*[3]
>
> —Rudyard Kipling

on the bench was a draft pick from 2000, Tom Brady. With star quarterback Drew Bledsoe already in the fold, the team figured it could wait for Brady's skinny body to fill out in the weight room. Over his first year he quietly developed his body and his game, preparing for an opportunity he saw as inevitable.

Georgia's Richard Seymour wasn't seen as the difference maker New England needed to find in the 2001 draft. He proved a lot of people wrong.

There were early signs that Brady was special. During a break in the weight room between the 2000 and 2001 seasons, he told receiver David Patten how to adjust some of his routes on the fly. Patten had already played NFL football for several years and was stunned that a rookie backup had that level of insight.[4]

By the summer of 2001, the Patriots had turned over the roster. A remarkable sixty-five of the eighty-eight players invited to training camp were brought in by Belichick and Pioli. The team had made wholesale changes at the pivotal linebacker position. Of the seventeen veterans signed that year, seven were starters that season, five were top subs, and another three were key performers on special teams. Far from being in salary cap trouble, the Patriots now had the third-lowest payroll in the league. It didn't look like they were ready to take the league by storm.

Nor did the 2001 season get off to an auspicious start. In week two, quarterback Drew Bledsoe suffered a jarring hit along the

Many Passed Over the Best Ever

As a Michigan Wolverine, Brady won 20 of the 25 games he started, facing top-tier competition such as Ohio State and Alabama, but was never "the guy." Even in Brady's senior year he split time with the much-hyped Drew Henson. Brady became a Patriot because the team valued football IQ and leadership qualities over physical traits. Famously, six quarterbacks were taken before Brady in the 2000 draft. QB coach Dick Rehbein, whose heart condition claimed his life before Brady's breakout, pushed the team to take him. The 2001 season was dedicated to Rehbein.

sidelines. His injury, which was serious, forced Tom Brady into the game. As a rookie in 2000, Brady threw one pass, a six-yard completion in the final moments of a blowout loss at Detroit, so his readiness to play was not a sure thing. No one knew it at the time, but Drew Bledsoe would never start another game for New England. Brady seized the job and never let go.

Brady's first NFL start was against the 2–0 Indianapolis Colts. Speaking to the media that week, the quarterback was confident and reminded everyone that he'd played in front of crowds of more than one hundred thousand at Michigan. His genial, slightly goofy tone alternated between humility and cockiness. A far cry from Belichick's laconic demeanor, Brady charmed reporters (and the world) then and now.

In the game, Brady's play was pedestrian but the veteran team around him came through. New England's defense picked off Peyton Manning four times, returning two of those interceptions for touchdowns. The game ended in a 44–13 win. Brady struggled in a loss to the Dolphins but the following week he engineered a come-from-behind win over San Diego. The Patriots then won three in a row, improving their record to 5–4.

New England's next opponent was St. Louis. Though they lost, the Patriots hung with the Rams and St. Louis's offensive mastermind, Mike Martz, predicted that the Pats would represent the AFC in the Super Bowl.

He was right.

6

CINDERELLA WORE SILVER AND BLUE

- - - - - - - - - - - -

In March 2001, Drew Bledsoe had signed the largest contract in league history, though it was more Kraft than Belichick who wanted to commit to him. When Bledsoe first returned from injury in late November, Belichick told him he could compete to start. A week later, he announced that Brady would be the starter for the rest of the season. This didn't sit well with the veteran, obviously, but Belichick disputed Bledsoe's assertion that he was lied to. "I don't feel like I misled him," said Belichick. "I really don't...I understood he wanted to play...He was a hardworking guy, he had been in the organization a long time, and I respected that. Nobody wanted him to get hurt and miss two months...You don't take a player who

With the emergence of Tom Brady, Drew Bledsoe
suddenly went from franchise passer to benchwarmer.

hasn't played in two months and then just stick him back in there
like nothing had happened."[1]

Even when Brady threw
interceptions in a rocky
thirteen-quarter stretch
of the season, Belichick
stuck with him. Two-thirds

> "It's never easy when you're the
> guy, then all of a sudden
> somebody else has your job."[2]
>
> —Drew Bledsoe

Belichick Gives Back

The coach's charitable giving has taken many forms over the years, from backing Jim Brown's Amer-I-Can program to establishing the Bill Belichick Foundation in 2014. The nonprofit provides coaching, mentorship, and financial support to individuals, communities, and organizations. Focusing on football and lacrosse, its mission is to bring the values of the Belichick family—a love of sports, coaching, and team-building—to the athletic leaders of tomorrow. Belichick and his family award high school seniors college scholarships, support youth sports organizations, and fund lacrosse and football clinics.

of the locker room stood by their coach's decision. They felt Bledsoe hung onto the ball too long, something Brady didn't do, and they admired the youngster's ultra-competitive nature. The other third felt Belichick had broken an unwritten rule of the NFL, which was that you couldn't lose your job due to injury. Some didn't like the implications of their coach benching a proven veteran with a $100-million contract. It meant no one's job was safe, no matter what they'd accomplished in the past.

A team player, Bledsoe advised and counseled Brady throughout the season. He genuinely liked the guy, which made it easier for him to accept what had happened and back Brady.

The team ended the regular season with a win over Miami. By then it was clear how much Belichick had changed. He was no longer the inflexible young coach who cursed out his players in Cleveland, less than a decade earlier. He knew he had earned the respect of this group. Entering the 2001 playoffs he was warm with his players and able to celebrate their accomplishment. "He learned a big lesson in becoming more of a players' coach,"[3] said Patriots' punter Ken Walter, who as a ballboy in Cleveland thought the Browns' locker room hated Belichick.

LEARNING TO TRUST HIS TEAM

In addition to taking a lighter touch with the players, Belichick acknowledged that he'd let go of the little things and learned to trust the people around him. "Being able to delegate and have confidence that other people are going to handle things and get it done is a really big step," he said, "because I like to be involved in the details and all that. But I've found out, I think there are a lot of people—when I delegate—who do a better job of doing it than I would have, anyway."[4]

In the playoffs, New England faced a Raiders team on the rise. Oakland had fallen just short of the Super Bowl in 2000 and would get there in 2003. In January 2002, the Patriots hosted the Raiders for a low-scoring affair played in blizzard conditions. Trailing 13–10 late in the fourth quarter, the Patriots' season looked like it was over when Raiders cornerback (and future Hall-of-Famer) Charles Woodson sacked Brady in the process of throwing the ball. To most it looked like a fumble, recovered by the Raiders. After an automatic review, referee Walt Coleman invoked the obscure "Tuck Rule" and declared the result of the play an incomplete pass. Twelve years later, the league would change the rule.

After the game, Brady stopped just short of acknowledging that he'd fumbled. "It was really a very fortunate call…But we took advantage of it." [5]

While the Raiders were deflated by this turn of events, Belichick had taught his team to remain focused on the job at hand, no matter what. Brady drove downfield as the snow continued to fall. The drive stalled again at the 29-yard line, bringing on a young, unproven kicker best known for chasing down former track star

> *"That's the worst call in the history of all sports."* [6]
>
> —Charles Woodson

Herschel Walker on a 1996 kickoff return in his rookie year, something kickers don't do. Though Adam Vinatieri had booted eight game winners in his first five seasons, three in 2001 alone, this was a do-or-die moment with an extremely high degree of difficulty. The 45-yard attempt would be taken in the face of swirling wind, on an icy playing surface.

Vinatieri's low kick didn't look like it had a chance. Somehow it arced over the heads of the flailing, slipping Raiders and split the uprights to tie the game at 13. Then, in overtime Brady orchestrated a 15-play, 61-yard drive that culminated in another Vinatieri field goal, this one for the win. It was a game that Raider Nation would lament to the end of their days, while Pats fans saw it as

Tom Brady and the Patriots might have missed their first trip to the Super Bowl were it not for a disputed call by the officiating crew on this Charles Woodson hit.

justice balancing the scales after the 1976 Raiders beat them on a questionable roughing-the-passer call and went on to win their first Super Bowl.

Leading up to the AFC championship versus Pittsburgh, Belichick used a comment from Steelers coach Bill Cowher to fire up his team. Cowher said the Steelers had already made their travel plans for the

Super Bowl, with the implication being that they'd looked past the Patriots. It was common practice to make arrangements contingent on victory, but Belichick knew that the perception of disrespect is a powerful motivator.

A Bill Belichick favorite, Troy Brown came up big against the Steelers. The veteran had gone from a roster long shot to the team's Swiss army knife. He did whatever was asked of him, and he did it well, even in high-pressure situations. Brown had emerged as Brady's favorite target in 2001. His 101 catches earned him Pro Bowl honors, but it was his skill with kick returns that Belichick called upon in the AFC Championship Game.

Belichick had been a special teams coach with Denver, Detroit, and the Giants. He knew the third phase of the game didn't get much respect, but it could be a tipping point in a close game. He allowed his special teams coach to use offensive and defensive starters on kickoffs and punts, something seldom done due to the risk of injury. That year Troy Brown had run back two punts for touchdowns and now, against Pittsburgh, he did it again in the first half. New England's specialists shone in the third quarter, blocking a Pittsburgh field goal attempt and returning it for the game-sealing score.

UPSET OF THE CENTURY

The Patriots entered their first Super Bowl under Bill Belichick as the second-biggest underdogs in the game's history. Two years earlier, the St. Louis Rams had won it all, and they felt confident this was a dynasty in the making. Dubbed "the Greatest Show on Turf," their high-flying offense had scored more than 500 points three year in a row, the first time a team had ever done that.

Meanwhile, their East Coast opponents were the Little Engine That Could. They had only three Pro Bowlers—Brady, Troy Brown, and safety Lawyer Milloy—an amazingly low number for a Super Bowl team. It was clear that collectively, the team's whole was greater than the sum of its parts. That whole was led by a nucleus of players who knew their roles in Belichick's system and had absolute confidence in it.

For the team introductions portion of the television broadcast, the Rams' players came out individually, with each player enjoying his time in the spotlight. The Patriots came out en masse, a show of unity and togetherness that struck a chord with the media and viewers alike. Five months after 9/11, it was easy to embrace the Patriots as "America's Team," a scrappy and resilient group of lunch-pail warriors without stars or outsized egos. They were the right team for the moment, and no one outside of St. Louis was rooting against them. It was a far cry from the attitude of much of the sports world just a few years later, when Belichick's juggernaut was compared to Darth Vader's Galactic Empire, the mafia, and worse.

The Patriots still had to win the game, of course, and it seemed like an impossible task. Just as he had against Buffalo, a decade earlier, Belichick concocted a plan to shut down a powerhouse offense.

Instead of blitzing star quarterback Kurt Warner, as they had in their regular season loss earlier that year, the Patriots focused on bumping Warner's weapons out of their precise timing patterns. Running back Marshall Faulk was the main target. The Patriots' linebackers, those smart, speedy overachievers, always kept track of Faulk, knocking him around whenever he released on a pass pattern. New England's physical play disrupted the Rams' offensive flow and kept their vaunted passing game out of rhythm. They blitzed the quarterback just once in the first half, but it was a doozy. Mike Vrabel came hard from Warner's right side, rushing his throw. Cornerback Ty Law picked off the errant pass and returned it 47 yards for the game's first touchdown. New England took an improbable 7–3 lead into the second quarter.

Just as he had in the Giants' Super Bowl victory over the Buffalo Bills, Belichick decided to let the other team run the ball if they wanted to. With their multiple defensive backs, his defenses presented looks that a team could run on with ease, practically begging Warner to hand off the ball to Faulk. But the Rams didn't take the bait. They tried to stick to their plan of pass, pass, pass. For the game Faulk had only seventeen carries for 76 yards.

This air-centric approach did allow New England to control the tempo of the game and hang with the Rams. In fact, the game was tied with 1:21 on the clock in the fourth quarter. As he had all year, Brady drove the team downfield with a series of short passes. A 23-yarder to Troy Brown put the Pats on the Rams' 36-yard line with twenty-three seconds left. Brady took one more shot to get in Adam Vinatieri's range, completing a 6-yarder to set up a 47-yard field goal. Vinatieri drilled it—his kick would have been good from a full 60 yards—and suddenly New England was an unlikely world champion, winning 20–17.

7

THE PATRIOT WAY

- - - - - - - - - - - - - - - -

In April 2002, the Patriots shipped Drew Bledsoe to Buffalo for a first-round pick. As the season unfolded, the free agents who were signed to complement the championship team flopped and the team overall showed signs of slipping. Where the hardly dominant 2001 team had been clutch, this group couldn't get to the big moments, let alone execute in them. After a 3–0 start, they lost four in a row. The defending champions just didn't have the same intensity and hunger for victory they felt as challengers.

Still, New England was in the playoff hunt till the end. If they beat Miami in week seventeen and the Packers defeated the Jets, the Patriots would make the playoffs. They held up their end of the bargain, winning a thrilling overtime game on yet another Vinatieri kick, but New York beat Green Bay and that was that.

After Belichick identified special teams as the Steelers' fatal flaw, punt returner Troy Brown made them pay in the 2002 AFC Championship Game.

Belichick wrote an op-ed for the *New York Times* on Super Bowl Sunday, titled "OK Champ, Now Comes the Hard Part." He reminded the winner that oftentimes the toughest job would be dealing with the post–Super Bowl hangover. "You'll tiptoe on the line between helping your players forget that they're the champions and helping them remember why they're the champions,"[1] he wrote.

WINNERS NEVER QUIT

Though Belichick did his best to recapture the magic of 2001, he quickly came to appreciate how difficult it was to maintain his players' intensity after winning a Super Bowl. The championship team had done it as hungry underdogs who played with a chip on their shoulders. This spirit was epitomized by Brady and Troy Brown, sixth- and eighth-round picks, and Adam Vinatieri, who wasn't even drafted. When they became champions, the squad lost that spirit, collectively if not to a man. They thought they could "flip a switch" and play at the same level they had before, in crunch time, but when the switch flipped it was too late. Belichick resolved to figure out a way to prevent this, should he be so fortunate as to win another Super Bowl.

Belichick favorite Lawyer Milloy was released in 2003 because he wouldn't accept a pay cut. There were no sacred cows in New England's ever-thrifty, always-unsentimental organization. This and other cost-cutting maneuvers over the previous three seasons allowed New England enough room under

Still Kicking

Adam Vinatieri is one of the only NFL placekickers to earn a number of nicknames in his career. "Mr. Clutch," "Automatic Adam," and "Iceman" are all fair handles for the player who has made game-winners in two Super Bowls and numerous last-minute situations. Vinatieri is likely to own the records for field goals attempted and made before he hangs up his cleats. Though he left the Patriots to join Indianapolis in 2006, the team has not issued his number 4 jersey to another player.

the salary cap to overhaul the team's inconsistent defensive backfield. Fiery veteran Rodney Harrison and coveted rookies Asante Samuel and Eugene Wilson stepped in as immediate upgrades.

At first, it seemed that the 2003 team would be crushed by injuries. But Belichick had built a very deep team. The talent at the top of the roster might not be among the league's best, but they were considerably stronger through the middle and at the bottom of the roster. A turning point came in October with a huge win over Tennessee, at the time a perennial Super Bowl contender. Belichick's squad closed the season on a 12–0 streak and wouldn't lose again for more than a year.

Because key players signed cut-rate deals to stay in New England, Belichick and Scott Pioli could attract better-than-average players with only slightly above-average contracts. The players who were second and third on the depth chart tended to be better than their counterparts on other teams. In 2003, injuries forced Belichick to use forty-two different starters and a total of sixty-five players, but it didn't sink the season. The subs stepped up and made plays at key moments.

In the AFC Championship Game, New England shut down Peyton Manning and the Colts. Backup quarterback Damon Huard did a masterful Peyton impression for the practice

> *"We're getting better. We're grinding out. We're getting there."*[2]
>
> —Bill Belichick

squad and earned a game ball, a very rare honor for a player who didn't log a minute of game time. Two years later, the Patriots were back in the Super Bowl.

This time, the NFC representative was the underdog. The Carolina Panthers were overachievers, an expansion team turned title contender in just eight years of existence. The game turned into a shootout, score knotted at 29 with under two minutes to play. "We're not going to lose this game," Ty Law said to safety Rodney Harrison, whose right arm was in a cast after a fourth-quarter injury sidelined him. "You know why? Because we have Tom Brady."[3]

Brady took the field. This drive was eerily similar to the one to beat the Rams. It ended when Vinatieri banged a 41-yarder through the uprights. New England had won its fifteenth game in a row, despite a league-high number of injuries. The team was now a measuring stick that other franchises were judged by. The culture Belichick had created was the gold standard in sports.

But at the same time, David had become Goliath. They'd won two out of three Super Bowls, if only by the slimmest of margins (six total points). The Patriots didn't have a colorful cast of high-profile characters, as that was the last thing their head coach wanted. In the "me-me-me" world of professional sports, the Patriots were an anomaly. They craved success as much as anyone, but even their best players seemed happy to keep their names out of the headlines. From the top down, the team philosophy was that drawing attention to yourself was vanity at best and, at worst, a distraction that could threaten everything they were working toward. The most unforgiveable sin was giving other teams the motivational fodder Belichick used so well when the other side provided it. Years later, Wes Welker got in hot water with his coach when in a press conference he made teasing references to the personal life of Jets coach Rex Ryan. That was a big no-no in Foxboro.

The team's monochromatic identity left some cold, even before scandals seemed to turn the world against them. Even then, Belichick used any sign of resentment to motivate the team's next season of dominance. This time they would be ready to defend their championship.

A SURGE OF STAR POWER

In 2004, Belichick and Pioli broke the mold a bit, acquiring a player who did not fit the profile of a team-first, happy-to-stay-quiet soldier. Cincinnati running back Corey Dillon had vocally criticized both the organization and his teammates. By then, though, the Patriots had the structure in place to support a potentially combustible personality like Dillon. The stable, unified organization and veteran leadership in the locker room encouraged the talented tailback to embrace "the Patriot Way."

Convinced it was the right move, the team acquired Dillon for a second-round draft pick, and the ex-Bengal turned over a new leaf in his new home. Dillon gave the ground game a power and consistency it had lacked in the past, improving the offense as a whole.

Running back Corey Dillon was a star for the Cincinnati Bengals, but it wasn't until he joined the Patriots that he found his home in the NFL.

New England was held under twenty points just once all season. The team won its nineteenth game in a row in October, breaking an NFL record, and entered the playoffs 14–2 on the year.

Once again facing Peyton Manning's Colts in the playoffs, the new-look Patriots dominated with the ground game as Dillon rolled up 144 rushing yards and kept the high-powered Indy offense off the field. New England controlled the ball for almost thirty-eight of the game's sixty minutes, coasting to victory that week and again in the AFC Championship Game against Pittsburgh.

What they call in sports "bulletin board material" came up again before the 2004 Super Bowl. The night before the game, Belichick showed his team every street and turn of the parade route the Philadelphia Eagles had planned if they won. Infuriated by this perceived slight, the players were properly fired up for the game.

Belichick's third Super Bowl as a head coach played out a bit differently than the first two. Instead of Brady driving for game-winning points in the last two minutes, it was the opposition who was forced to mount a comeback. The Eagles drew within three points with 1:55 to play. New England failed to run out the clock and Philly regained possession with fifty-five seconds left. This time it was Eagles quarterback Donovan McNabb driving for the winning points. But Rodney Harrison secured a deflected pass and clinched the victory with his dramatic interception. Belichick shared a moment of celebration with his father, Steve, before linebacker Tedy Bruschi dumped water on the both of them.

With the victory, Belichick became the only NFL head coach to win three Super Bowls in four years.

In 2006–2007, Manning and the Colts finally beat their nemesis in the playoffs. Indianapolis came back from a 21–3 deficit, exposing weaknesses in the Patriots that would have

"I think Tom [Brady] is one of the most consistent players that I've ever coached."[4]

—Bill Belichick

Who's Better?

Between 2001 and 2015, Tom Brady and Peyton Manning developed a friendly rivalry as each made his case for being considered the greatest quarterback of all time. Though Brady led their head-to-head series 11–6, Manning went 3–2 in their playoff meetings. Manning finished his career 14–13 in the playoffs, with two Super Bowl rings, while Brady is 27–10 and has five rings. Of course, those are team accomplishments. Individually Peyton was a five-time NFL MVP and seven-time first-team NFL All-Pro, while Tom has earned those honors three times. He's on pace to break most of Manning's career passing records.

to be addressed. Brady threw a backbreaking interception while driving for a potentially game-winning score. A shootout for the ages ended as a 38–34 win for Indy.

That year Tom Brady did a masterful job with little in the way of weapons, but New England was in desperate need of upgrades in its receiving corps. Over the last few seasons there had been a lot of turnover on the roster. Belichick wanted to keep the team stocked with young talent because such players were usually playing for their first Super Bowl ring, their second contract—usually the biggest payday in a player's career—or both. What's more, young players were almost always less expensive to acquire than battle-tested veterans. This allowed the Patriots to stockpile such players rather than having a top-heavy roster like the Colts', which was weighed down by Manning's huge contract.

The downside to Belichick's strategy with personnel was that many steady and reliable players departed, signing larger deals elsewhere or drifting toward retirement. Sometimes the Patriots' desired depth wasn't there. In the 2005 and 2006 seasons, draft misfires hurt them and the new guard didn't step up.

In 2007, however, Belichick restocked Brady's arsenal. As an undrafted free agent best known for shining on special teams, receiver Wes Welker was a typical Patriots acquisition that would pay off handsomely. Randy Moss had pouted and went half speed during a dismal season for the Raiders, so the wildly talented wideout was available cheap—it required just a fourth-round pick for New England to acquire him. The move was reminiscent of the Corey Dillon trade. Though considered a malcontent in Oakland, Moss was given a clean slate at Foxboro.

With these major offensive acquisitions, the table was now set for a historic run. But storm clouds were brewing, as well.

8

A TARNISHED LEGACY?

- - - - - - - - - - - - - - - - - -

New England entered the 2007 season on a mission. In the season opener, the Patriots' explosive offense made huge plays in a 38–14 win over the Jets. But the world's attention quickly shifted from the scoreboard to the sideline, where a Patriots videographer was found recording the hand signals used by Jets' defensive coaches. "Spygate" would become one of the biggest controversies in NFL history.

It was common, even accepted, for a team to try to decipher opponents' hand signals. Knowing this, coaches display "dummy" signals in addition to real ones. But capturing signals with a camera for later study crossed a line in the eyes of many. A cascade of criticism came crashing down on the Patriots and Belichick personally. The validity of victories was called into question and words like "cheating" were thrown around. Officially, the league punished the Patriots by taking

During the 2007 season, the Patriots celebrated sixty-seven offensive touchdowns, including this September score by receiver Wes Welker.

away a first-round draft pick and issuing hefty fines to the team and to Belichick. Unofficially, resentment was widespread, rumors swirled, and wild accusations were made.

Within the organization, it was all just fuel for the fire. Belichick had long used the disrespect of others to inspire his team, and in this case the players rallied to his defense. Their view was that if from

Unfair Advantages

While the Patriots' misdeeds have received the largest penalties and most attention, most teams have incurred league discipline for various offenses: pumping fake crowd noise into the stadium, coaches impeding the progress of ball carriers running along the sideline, the use of Stickum adhesive to improve players' grip, salary cap manipulation, faking injuries to stop the clock, taking performance-enhancing drugs, secretly negotiating contracts, rewarding defenders for injuring offensive players, and more. In 2010, ex-Patriots Steve Scarnecchia and Josh McDaniels were punished for the Denver Broncos' videotaping offense.

now on they beat every opponent by the largest margin possible, scoring in historic numbers, it would prove that the team was just that good. It would show the world they clearly didn't need to steal a team's signals to beat them.

A TOUGH YEAR

And that's exactly how the 2007 season went, for the most part. It was a series of blowouts. Almost every week Brady found Randy Moss deep for a long scoring strike, or perhaps two.

Late in the year, though, there were warning signs. The victory margins shrank as defenses that could pressure Brady gave the Patriots problems. Though he tried to conceal a foot injury, he was photographed wearing a walking boot. Still, New England completed its perfect regular season with a win over the Giants, setting a number of records including most wins in one season (16), touchdown passes (50), touchdown receptions (23 for Moss), total touchdowns (75), and most points (589).

Matched up with the Giants in the Super Bowl, the undefeated Patriots were overwhelming favorites. The pressure to win only mounted when Spygate resurfaced in a pair of newspaper articles published the day before the game, one voicing suspicions that the Patriots had taped the Rams' final walk-through, just prior to their first Super Bowl win. "I really felt it [pressure] leading up to the game," said long-time Patriot Tedy Bruschi. "It's supposed to be just about playing the game and executing your assignment and doing those things. But I mean, you're in the midst of a year where everyone is questioning your head coach, and the validity of your world championships are questioned. It's the most pressure I've ever felt in my entire career."[1]

In the first half the Giants attacked Brady relentlessly, bringing more blitzes than in their week seventeen meeting. The quarterback was sacked four times in three quarters of play. Entering the fourth, the Patriots' high-octane offense hadn't even hit double digits on the scoreboard. With New England clinging to a 7–3 lead, Giants QB Eli Manning (Peyton's younger brother) connected with receiver David Tyree on a short touchdown pass. The world knew an upset might be brewing. But Brady answered with a methodical drive that culminated with a Moss touchdown to retake the lead.

This left Manning about two and a half minutes to work with. Making one of the most memorable plays in Super Bowl history, he found Tyree in the middle of the field for a 32-yard gainer. To make the contested catch over Rodney Harrison, Tyree pinned the ball against his facemask and held it firm. The drive continued. With sixty seconds left, Belichick called a desperation blitz but it didn't reach Manning in time. Plaxico Burress reeled in a 13-yard touchdown pass, Brady was sacked for the fifth time, and the Giants won 17–14. It was the greatest upset in Super Bowl history.

The *Boston Herald* would print a retraction of its story about the Patriots taping the Rams' walk-through, and the Spygate talk finally subsided in 2008. Belichick had the team ready to bounce back from the crushing disappointment of the Super Bowl setback. But seven and a half minutes into the season, disaster struck. Tom Brady was hit low by Kansas City Chiefs' safety Bernard Pollard. Brady screamed, gripping his knee. He would be diagnosed with a torn ACL and was out for the year.

Backup Matt Cassel would play exceptionally well for a seventh-round draft pick who had never even started a game in college. As the year went along, the fourth-year pro learned to avoid mistakes. In the team's last three games, Cassel threw seven touchdowns to just one interception. Despite finishing 11–5, New England missed the playoffs on a tiebreaker. Ironically, Cassel was traded to the Chiefs when Brady returned, but he never enjoyed the same level of success he did in the Patriots' system.

Also joining the Chiefs in 2009 was Scott Pioli. It was hard for Belichick to say good-bye, but he understood that this was a promotion for Pioli. They were good friends who'd discussed every aspect of

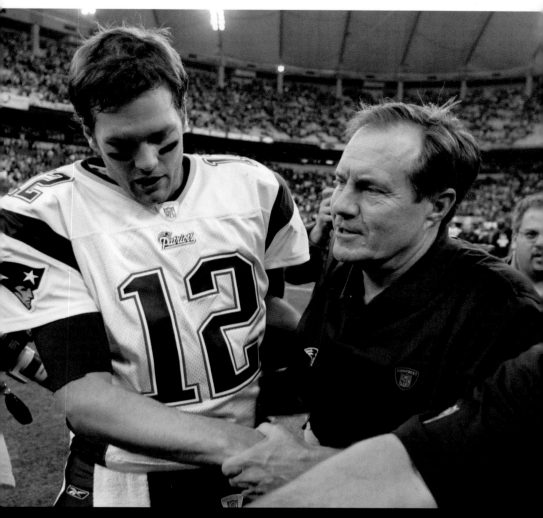

Belichick and Brady had to regroup after a heartbreaking loss to the Giants in the 2008 Super Bowl. The next two years were tough.

their team's football operations from the very beginning. Now Pioli could put his own stamp on rebuilding a team.

It was also time for another dyed-in-the-wool Patriot to move on. When Tedy Bruschi retired, Belichick came as close to crying as anyone had seen publicly. "He's the perfect player," Belichick said in a voice that shook and cracked. "He has helped create a tradition here that we're all proud of."[2]

With Bruschi's retirement and the trade of Richard Seymour, the Patriots lost players who were essentially extensions of Belichick on the field. They had compiled a 111–34 record in their Patriots career together. Brady's return was the only encouraging sign entering the 2009 season.

In November, Belichick's decision making was criticized in the media when, in a primetime duel with their old rivals the Indianapolis Colts, his daring play call backfired. With the Patriots leading by six with two minutes to play and the ball at their own twenty-eight, Belichick went for it on fourth and two rather than punt the ball away. They came up short, gave Peyton Manning a short field, and lost by a point when the Colts scored a touchdown. Conventional wisdom was to punt inside your own 30-yard-line, especially with the lead, needing more than a yard to get the first down. Statistical analysis showed that, at worst, Bill's decision was just as likely to work out as punting.[3]

Regardless, it was a bad omen. That season the Patriots would suffer their first home playoff loss of the Belichick and Brady era. On the first play from scrimmage, Baltimore Ravens tailback Ray Rice sprinted 83 yards for a touchdown, setting the table for a 24–0 first quarter and a 33–14 victory. This was not how a Patriots season was supposed to end, and Belichick did a lot of soul searching in the weeks and months to follow.

WHEELING AND DEALING

And yet, Belichick embraced the challenge to get back on top. The team-building process itself excited him, from the big picture to the tiniest detail. He never complained of burnout or the need for a break from coaching, at least not publicly. At an age (fifty-eight) where many consider retirement, Belichick got to work on the next phase for his Patriots.

Like a shrewd fantasy football owner, Belichick liked to move up and down in the NFL Draft (usually down), adding extra picks in the process. He paid close attention to what other teams thought of players and what leaked into

Game Changer

Though Bill Belichick is regarded as a defensive coach, his offensive innovations are numerous. Most NFL teams try to follow the same winning formula week after week, doing whatever it is they do best. Belichick adapts each week's game plan for the opponent. If they're tough against the run, he'll pass almost every play. If the next opponent has a weak run defense, he'll call run after run. Belichick's creative use of two tight-end sets in the passing game has been widely imitated. In the 2014 playoffs, he confused the Baltimore Ravens by having offensive players report as ineligible receivers.

the media about their plans. There were often players Belichick and his scouts liked better than other teams did, and this gave them a chance to trade back a few spots, turning a profit and still getting the player they wanted. "If you don't feel there's that big of a market for the player, you can back off a bit if you have the chance, and accumulate picks,"[4] Bill explained.

For example, in the 2010 draft Belichick swung two trades to move down a total of five spots in the first round. In return the Patriots moved up from the fourth round to the third and gained another fourth. Belichick still got his guy, defensive back Devin McCourty. McCourty would have a long and productive career in New England. The extra picks obtained in this kind of deal often became meaningful contributors to the team.

The new-look Patriots were nearly as effective on offense as the record-breaking 2007 team. While Moss was traded to the Minnesota Vikings, a pair of rookie tight ends, Rob Gronkowski and Aaron Hernandez, gave defenses fits. They were too big for safeties to deal with and too fast for linebackers to cover. Meanwhile, the slippery Wes Welker had blossomed into an ideal short-range target for Brady, setting a number of records in the course of his Patriots career.

New England opened the year 10–2. However, one of the teams to defeat them was Cleveland, whose defense was then coached by Rob Ryan. Rob's brother Rex was the head coach of the Jets. Rob shared his strategy for

> *"I don't Twitter, I don't MyFace, I don't Yearbook. I don't do any of those things."*[5]
>
> —Bill Belichick

slowing the Patriots offense, and it was even more effective for the Jets, whose roster was much more talented than the Browns'. The division rivals squared off in the playoffs, with the Patriots a huge home favorite. But the Jets showed Brady unpredictable fronts, mixing man and zone coverages, and made big plays on offense. The outcome was a shocking 28–21 win for New York.

9

ON TO CINCINNATI

- - - - - - - - - - - - - - - - -

O ver the course of a decade, Belichick had patiently built a pro-
gram in New England. Since taking the job in 2000 he had made
draft-day deals with twenty-four of the league's thirty-two franchises.
All that maneuvering had borne fruit again; despite finishing 2010
with the NFL's best record, New England had multiple early-round
picks in the 2011 draft. Bill likes to use his first-round pick and trade
the second, usually for a future selection. He would do it again, draft-
ing tackle Nate Solder with the pick acquired in the Richard Seymour
trade and then trading down for a future first. Solder would become
a mainstay of the offensive line for years to come.

The 2011 team was another point-scoring machine, but the defense
was suspect. The Patriots scored thirty-six points per game in a

Belichick's crudely customized sweatshirts make him stand out on the sidelines, and some say his choices might even influence the outcome of games.

season-closing eight-game winning streak, as tight ends Gronkowski and Hernandez ran roughshod through defenses. The Patriots faced the Ravens in the conference championship with an opportunity to heal the wounds of their home playoff loss in 2009. One of Bill's bottom-of-the-roster gems, a rookie free agent named Sterling Moore, batted away a ball that would have been the game-winning catch and New England advanced to their first Super Bowl in four years. Once again, their opponents were the New York Giants.

Once again, the Giants would pull out an improbable victory. This time they came back from a 17–9 deficit. With Gronkowski hobbled by an injury suffered versus the Ravens, Belichick's two-tight-end attack was less effective. Wes Welker dropped a critical pass. Meanwhile, Eli Manning threaded a difficult throw down the sideline to receiver Mario Manningham, and Ahmad Bradshaw capitalized with a game-winning touchdown.

THE GOING GETS TOUGHER

The following year, the Ravens again put an end to the Patriots' season, knocking out New England in the AFC

Boy in the Hood

Bill Belichick is called "the Hoodie" because of his habit of wearing hooded sweatshirts on the sidelines, often with their restrictive sleeves unevenly sheared off for the comfort of what he's acknowledged are short arms. Mike Dussault of PatsProgapanda.com has tracked Belichick's clothing choices since he unveiled (or veiled himself in) his first hoodie, in 2003. It seems that gray is the coach's best bet, as his record in that color was 32–9 entering the 2017 season.

Championship Game. After the season, the team found itself in transition again. Gronk underwent surgery, Wes Welker departed in free agency, and shockingly, Aaron Hernandez was arrested for the murder of Odin Lloyd, a player for the Boston Bandits, a New England-based semi-pro football team.

Belichick addressed the Hernandez case hours after releasing the troubled tight end. "We've worked very hard together over the past fourteen years to put together a winning team that is a pillar in the community...My comments are certainly not in proportion to the unfortunate and sad situation that we have here. But I've been advised to address the situation once, and it's time for the New England Patriots to move forward."[1]

For Belichick, any time something bad happened, whether it was a loss, an injury, or a tragedy, the phrase "move forward" would quickly be invoked. And the team

> *"Twenty-four hours after the game, you gotta' move on."*[2]
>
> **—Bill Belichick**

did just that. However, the injury bug bit them again, and by the time New England faced the Denver Broncos in the AFC Championship, they had suffered significant losses on both sides of the ball. That year their old adversary Peyton Manning, now a Bronco, had broken most of Brady's single-season records from 2007. He threw for 400 yards to author a ten-point win.

Belichick often told his players to "ignore the noise," but public disdain for the Patriots had only grown after the Spygate scandal. Pundits noted that while the Patriots were winning more games than any team in the league, they had not won a Super Bowl since Spygate. Whether it could be attributed to injuries, "cosmic retribution," the team not taping coaches anymore, or the absence of a championship-caliber defense, many took pleasure in this fact, and not just fans of other teams in the AFC East. NFL commissioner Roger Goodell said in an interview that he felt "deceived" by Belichick in his Spygate apology. The world, and perhaps the league, seemed ready to punish the Patriots at the earliest opportunity.

That opportunity came the following winter. After an up-and-down regular season that saw some commentators bury Brady after a bad week-four loss in Kansas City, the Patriots rallied. It began with Belichick answering "We're on to Cincinnati" after virtually every question about the Kansas City loss, continued with a 43–17 romp in Cincinnati (the first of seven straight wins), and landed New England in yet another playoff tilt with the Colts, this one in the AFC Championship Game.

The most consequential thing to come out of the contest, other than the Patriots winning to advance to their fifth Super Bowl in the Belichick era, was seemingly inconsequential at the time. There had been talk in the media that season about the air pressure quarterbacks preferred in the footballs they threw. Green Bay's Aaron Rodgers had large hands and said he favored an overinflated football.

Tom Brady, it would be learned, wanted a ball that was on the lower end of the spectrum.

Even the most avid of football fans probably didn't know, at the time, what the league rules were for air pressure in a game ball. They were supposed to be kept between 12.5 and 13.5 per square inch (psi). Before the game, the Colts told the league that they wanted to make sure the twelve footballs used were kept at those specifications. Somehow the balls still wound up in a stadium bathroom twenty minutes before the game, where they went unsupervised for a period of time. At halftime eleven of twelve were found to be at least slightly underinflated.

A new controversy was born. Roger Goodell handed down a four-game suspension of Tom Brady that the quarterback would fight in court. Though Belichick was not penalized, the team was fined $1 million and stripped of first- and fourth-round draft picks.

THE DEFIANT ONES

Even with "Deflategate" dragging out over two seasons, the Patriots stayed focused. Arguably, they reached a level of play otherwise unattainable without the "us against the world" attitude the NFL discipline gave them. Fantasy owners would successfully employ "the Angry Tom Brady" strategy, believing that Belichick and Brady would keep their foot on the gas against other teams, as a way of sticking it to Goodell and the league. "We don't need to record sidelines or underinflate footballs to be dominant," their play seemed to say.

First, though, there was the 2015 Super Bowl to play. Defending champions Seattle had trounced the Denver Broncos the year before, and they presented Brady with a formidable defense. At halftime the score was knotted at fourteen and then Seattle pulled to a ten-point lead in the third quarter. As usual, though, Brady rallied. His touchdown toss to receiver Julian Edelman, the latest undrafted free agent to excel in a Patriots uniform, put New England up 28–24.

It was now up to the New England defense to fend off quarterback Russell Wilson, running back Marshawn Lynch, and a yards-devouring Seahawks attack. With twenty-six seconds left, Seattle was just steps from pay dirt. Rather than hand the ball to Lynch, the engine of the offense, Pete Carroll opted to surprise New England with a pass from the one yard line.

Ernie Adams, still a vital part of Belichick's brain trust, had done research suggesting that Seattle would run a play like this near the goal line. Belichick gave his cornerbacks specific instructions on how to defend it. "If

"Do Your Job"

Bill Belichick's mantra, "Do your job," is applicable in many situations. Obviously, it suggests accountability, as Patriots players take personal responsibility for their assignments. To do your job you must be prepared, detail oriented, and hard working. But Belichick also invokes the saying to remind his players that they don't have to worry about the media, or the score, or what the other team is doing. Just focus on your task at hand. If everyone does their job, more often than not the outcome for the team will be a win.

Moments after intercepting Tom Brady's pass in the 2015 AFC Championship Game, D'Qwell Jackson reported that this ball felt underinflated and the "Deflategate" investigation began.

you see that formation, you have to just jump it,"[3] Belichick said, meaning that they had to lunge underneath the receiver's route. In practices leading up to the game, Malcolm Butler screwed up and the result was a touchdown. He vowed that he wouldn't be beaten again.

Seeing the play unfold, Butler reacted the way he was supposed to, anticipating the throw and getting to the ball before Wilson's receiver could. The game-sealing interception capped off one of the most exciting Super Bowls played to date.

In 2015, the Patriots rolled to their fourth consecutive 12–4 record despite subpar play from Brady's blockers. The team's offensive line woes came to a head in the AFC championship, when a ferocious Denver Broncos pass rush battered Brady to the tune of twenty knockdowns and four sacks. The Pats could muster only thirty-one rushing yards. Peyton Manning, playing the second-to-last game of his storied career, did just enough offensively to eke out the 20–18 win.

As usual with Belichick, identifying an area to address in the off-season (the line) would soon be followed with a solution.

10

BELICHICK BURNISHES HIS CREDENTIALS

- - - - - - - - - - - - - - - - - -

Reliable offensive linemen don't exactly grow on trees, so Belichick took a different approach to the problem. Entering the 2016 season, Belichick coaxed Dante Scarnecchia out of retirement. After thirty years with the Patriots, fifteen as offensive line coach, "Scar" had retired in 2014. He was widely regarded as one of the greatest minds in his specialty, and his return made an immediate impact up front. Pro Football Focus, which grades players on their effectiveness in games, charted massive improvement in the same blockers who had struggled the previous year.

BACK ON TOP?

Even with Brady serving his Deflategate suspension for the first four games, New England opened the year 3–1 and finished 14–2. After decisive wins over the Houston Texans and Pittsburgh Steelers in the playoffs, the Patriots faced an Atlanta Falcons team that had the league's highest-scoring offense in 2016. Headed by league MVP Matt Ryan, that offense put the Pats in a 28–3 hole halfway through the third quarter. Thus began the greatest comeback of Tom Brady's career. Brady led three scoring drives, and the Patriots defense stymied the high-flying Falcons' attack.

Now down 28–20, the Patriots drove ninety-one yards in ten plays to make the score 28–26. On the ensuing two-point conversion attempt, slot receiver Danny Amendola took a Brady screen pass into the end zone to tie the game. Entering the first overtime period in Super Bowl history, the Patriots won the coin toss and got the first crack at scoring.

> *"There's no quarterback I'd rather have than Tom Brady. He's the best."*[1]
>
> —Bill Belichick

After four completed passes, a run, and pass interference against Atlanta, New England reached the two-yard line. The winning points were at hand, but Brady's first pass was errant. Then halfback James White took a toss to the right, leaped over the goal line and ended the game with a touchdown. The thrilling 34–28 victory meant a fifth

Pictured in 2006, long-time Patriots assistant coach Dante Scarnecchia came out of retirement to help the 2016 team cure their offensive line woes.

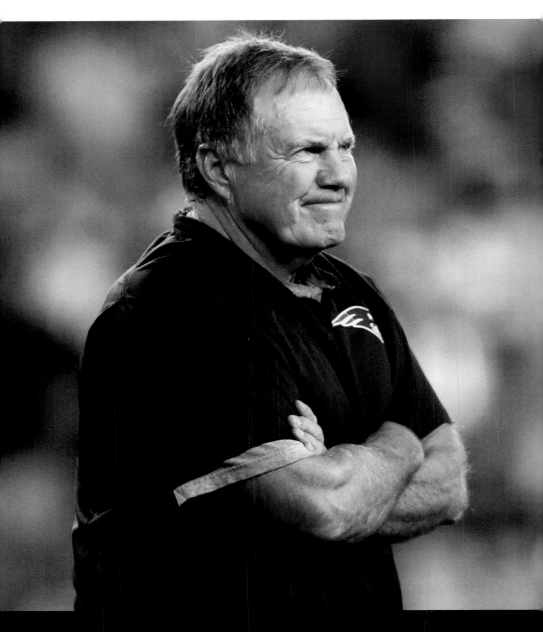

After all these years, Bill Belichick still lives and dies with his team on game day.

Lombardi Trophy for Belichick and Brady, cementing their claim to "greatest of all time" status. With the win they had won more Super Bowls than any coach or quarterback in history.

While much of the credit for taking Tom Brady must go to the late Dick Rehbein, the fact remains that in 2000 Belichick made a sixth-round draft choice that has provided arguably the greatest return on investment in modern history. And yet it speaks to the standards Belichick has set that the team viewed this as a failure of their player evaluation system. After all, Brady slipped through the cracks for 198 selections until New England took him. In Belichick's world, this was a lucky break they'd better learn from.

National Treasure

With the Patriots win over the Atlanta Falcons, the team increased its merchandise revenue by more than 50 percent. Purchased for $172 million in 1994, the franchise was now valued at $3.7 billion, second only to Jerry Jones's Dallas Cowboys ($4.8 billion). In 2012, only the Cowboys were worth $2 billion.

Would Belichick have won five Super Bowls if he'd drafted any of the six quarterbacks taken before Brady in 2000? The answer would seem to be no, but we'll never know for sure. Did Brady make Belichick or did Belichick make Brady? The coach has won games with Matt Cassel, Jimmy Garappolo, and Jacoby Brissett at the helm, but none were tested in the postseason. There is no question that Brady is one of the most cool-under-pressure

Bill, by the Numbers

After the 2018 season, Bill Belichick was sixty-seven wins behind Miami Dolphins coach Don Shula's all-time-record total of 328. No NFL team had a winning record against Belichick's Patriots. In 2018 New England became the only team in league history to win ten straight division championships. That win brought their total number of AFC East titles under Belichick up to sixteen. Belichick also set a record for coaching the most playoff games (forty-two) and playoff wins (thirty-one).

playoff quarterbacks in history.

Regardless, it's clear that the synergy between the two men is very, very special. In addition to his way with players, Belichick has formed highly effective partnerships with the right people time and time again: in New York, with Bill Parcells; in Cleveland, with Nick Saban; and in New England, with Robert Kraft and Scott Pioli. The common denominator is Belichick.

DON'T HATE THE HOODIE

Parcells sees no reason for Belichick's success to end. "As time goes on, I think, it's actually not harder, it's easier, because his experience is so much greater and he's been through two or three cycles of players, so he can reference back to the kinds of players that have been successful for him before and try to integrate similar ones into the system for the future," said Parcells. "That's what all of us basically try to do. If a player doesn't remind you of some other player that you had some success with, then there's probably a good chance that that player isn't going to be successful."[2]

These days, though, Belichick seems almost content. His girlfriend, Linda Holliday is, as he put it, "the rose next to the thorn." She sees a different side of him than the rest of us. "He can sing," she said. "And he can sing well. You won't hear it. You won't see it. But he can sing well."[3]

Holliday is the executive director of the Bill Belichick Foundation, which he credits her for starting. For years Belichick has awarded scholarships to handpicked students at his alma mater, Annapolis High School. The foundation expanded that work to also support students around the country and the world.

Whatever is next for Belichick, whether it's more Lombardi Trophies, more controversy, or perhaps a quieter end to his career, the coach has established a legacy that will stand the test of time. His imperfections, peculiarities, and occasionally poor fashion choices do not diminish the respect he's earned for doing the seemingly impossible in this day and age, as the architect of an NFL dynasty. Though Belichick is the first to say he's a football coach, nothing more, his unique application of teamwork, adaptability, and attention to detail is a model for success when facing any challenge.

CHRONOLOGY

- - - - - - - - - - - -

1952 William Stephen Belichick is born in Nashville, Tennessee.

1975 Belichick graduates from Wesleyan University with a degree in economics.

1975 After joining the Baltimore Colts as an intern, Belichick rapidly works his way up to his first paying position in the NFL.

1976 The Detroit Lions hire Belichick as a special teams assistant.

1978 Belichick joins the Denver Broncos' staff, focusing on special teams and defense.

1979 The New York Giants make Belichick their special teams coach.

1985 Giants coach Bill Parcells promotes Belichick to defensive coordinator.

1987 The Giants win Super Bowl XXI, defeating John Elway's Denver Broncos.

1991 The Giants edge the Buffalo Bills to win Super Bowl XXV. Belichick's defensive game plan is credited with slowing the Bills' high-powered offense.

1991 The Cleveland Browns give Belichick his first head-coaching job.

1995 After compiling a 36–44 record in Cleveland, Belichick is fired by owner Art Modell.

1996 Belichick rejoins Bill Parcells, now the head coach of the New England Patriots, as an assistant coach.

1997 Parcells brings Belichick to the New York Jets.

2000 Belichick turns down the Jets head-coaching job, and Patriots owner Robert Kraft hires him as head coach in New England.

2002 The Patriots upset the heavily favored St. Louis Rams in Super Bowl XXXVI.

2004 With four seconds on the clock, the Patriots kick a field goal to defeat the Carolina Panthers in Super Bowl XXXVIII.

2005 The Patriots defeat the Philadelphia Eagles in Super Bowl XXXIX, with Belichick becoming the first head coach to win three Super Bowls in four years.

2008 The New York Giants shock the Patriots in Super Bowl XLII, denying them the league's first nineteen-game unbeaten season.

2012 In Super Bowl XLVI, the Giants upset the Patriots once again, 21–17.

2015 With a last-second stop, the Patriots hold on to beat the Seattle Seahawks in Super Bowl XLIX.

2017 The Patriots rally from a 25-point third-quarter deficit to edge the Atlanta Falcons in Super Bowl LI, giving Belichick his fifth Super Bowl win as head coach.

2018 Super Bowl LII sees the scrappy Philadelphia Eagles claiming their first Super Bowl victory, defeating the Patriots 41–33.

2019 The Patriots beat the Los Angeles Rams in Super Bowl LIII.

CHAPTER NOTES

-- -- -- -- -- -- -- -- -- -- -- --

INTRODUCTION

1. Bella English, "After a Bruising Year, Belichick Opens Up," Boston.com, March 4, 2007, http://archive.boston.com/sports/football/patriots/articles/2007/03/04/after_a_bruising_year_belichick_opens_up/.

CHAPTER 1: BORN INTO A FOOTBALL FAMILY

1. David Halberstam, *The Education of a Coach* (New York, NY: Hachette Books, 2006), p. 73.
2. David Fleming, "No More Questions," ESPN.com, September 4, 2016, http://www.espn.com/espn/feature/story/_/id/17703210/new-england-patriots-coach-bill-belichick-greatest-enigma-sports.
3. Jeff Howe, "Bill Belichick Reflects on His Father's Impact on His Career, Says Football 'Was My Life as a Kid,'" New England

Sports Network, January 30, 2012, https://nesn.com/2012/01/bill-belichick-reflects-on-his-fathers-impact-on-his-career-says-football-was-my-life-as-a-kid/.

4. Robert Cocuzzo and Bruce A. Percelay, "Winning Combination," *N Magazine*, June 28, 2017, http://www.n-magazine.com/winning-combination/.

5. Halberstam, p. 99.

6. Dan Shaughnessy, "Is Little-Known Bill Belichick Confidant Ernie Adams the Secret to the Patriots' Success?" *Boston Globe*, January 29, 2015, https://www.bostonglobe.com/sports/2015/01/29/mysterious-ernie-adams-patriots-man-behind-curtain/IrNCfgrysUphGpkcIjEaBL/story.html.

CHAPTER 2: STUDENT OF THE GAME

1. David Halberstam, *The Education of a Coach* (New York, NY: Hachette Books, 2006), p. 104.

2. John Breech, "Irsay Thinks Highly of Belichick, Who Started Coaching Career with Colts," CBSSPORTS.com, October 18, 2015, https://www.cbssports.com/nfl/news/irsay-thinks-highly-of-belichick-who-started-coaching-career-with-colts/.

3. Dan Wetzel, "Bill Belichick Emotional Talking About the Late Ted Marchibroda," Yahoo.com, January 16, 2016, https://sports.yahoo.com/news/belichick-gets-emotional-talking-about-the-late-ted-marchibroda-045721242.html.

4. Halberstam, p. 122.

5. Bill Belichick, AZ Quotes, http://www.azquotes.com/ quote/700697.

6. Mike Wells, "Bill Belichick Got His Coaching Start with the Colts in 1975," ESPN.com, October 16, 2015, http:// www.espn.com/blog/indianapolis-colts/post/_/id/14194/ bill-belichick-got-his-coaching-start-with-the-colts-in-1975.

7. Michael Holley, *Patriot Reign* (New York, NY: HarperCollins, 2004), p. 13.

CHAPTER 3: A GIANT LEAP

1. Michael David Smith, "Bill Belichick: Lawrence Taylor Could Tell Who Was Blocking Him by the Fear in Their Eyes," Pro Football Talk, September 16, 2017, http://profootballtalk.nbcsports. com/2017/09/16/bill-belichick-lawrence-taylor-could-tell-who-was-blocking-him-by-the-fear-in-their-eyes/.

2. Ralph Vacchiano, "The Genius of Little Bill: Belichick's Super Bowl XXV Game Plan with Giants Is Stuff of Legend," *New York Daily News*, November 14, 2015, http://www.nydailynews.com/ sports/football/giants/bill-belichick-super-bowl-xxv-game-plan-stuff-legend-article-1,2435400.

3. David Halberstam, *The Education of a Coach* (New York, NY: Hachette Books, 2006), p. 173.

4. Michael Eisen, "Belichick's Gameplan," Giants.com, http://www. giants.com/25/article-belichick.html.

5. Vacchiano.

CHAPTER 4: BROKEN-HEARTED BROWNS

1. Vito Stellino, "Playing After Assassination Was Regrettable," *Baltimore Sun*, November 21, 1993, http://articles.baltimoresun. com/1993-11-21/sports/1993325149_1_modell-rozelle-cowboys/2.

2. Michael Holley, *Patriot Reign* (New York, NY: HarperCollins, 2004), p. 6.

3. David Fleming, "No More Questions," ESPN.com, September 4, 2016, http://www.espn.com/espn/feature/story/_/id/17703210/ new-england-patriots-coach-bill-belichick-greatest-enigma-sports.

4. Phil Perry, "Belichick, Saban Used to 'Sneak Out' to Concerts in Cleveland," CSN.NE.com, October 8 2016, http://www.csnne.com/new-england-patriots/ belichick-saban-used-sneak-out-concerts-cleveland.

5. Fleming.

6. Ibid.

7. Ibid.

8. Holley, p. 24.

9. Holley, p. 20.

10. George Vecsey, "Parcells Seeking New Kitchen," *New York Times*, February 1, 1997, http://www.nytimes.com/1997/02/01/sports/parcells-seeking-new-kitchen.html.

11. Judy Battista, "Patriots Hire Belichick, and Everyone's Happy," *New York Times*, January 28, 2000, http://www.nytimes.com/2000/01/28/sports/pro-football-patriots-hire-belichick-and-everyone-s-happy.html

12. Ibid.

13. Ibid.

CHAPTER 5: A NEW WAY TO WIN

1. Christopher Price, *The Blueprint* (New York, NY: Thomas Dunne Books, 2007), p. 3.

2. Michael Holley, *Patriot Reign* (New York, NY: HarperCollins, 2004), p. 23.

3. Rudyard Kipling, "The Law of the Jungle" (Poem).

4. Price, p. 198.

CHAPTER 6: CINDERELLA WORE SILVER AND BLUE

1. Michael Holley, *Patriot Reign* (New York, NY: HarperCollins, 2004), p. 47.

2. Michael Weinreb, "Holy Tuck," The Ringer, January 19, 2017, https://www.theringer.com/2017/1/19/16038422/nfl-playoffs-tuck-rule-oral-history-raiders-patriots-15-years-later-d731b0a6d00e.

3. Ibid.

4. Christopher Price, *The Blueprint* (New York, NY: Thomas Dunne Books, 2007), p. 149.

5. Weinreb.

6. Ibid.

CHAPTER 7: THE PATRIOT WAY

1. Christopher Price, *The Blueprint* (New York, NY: Thomas Dunne Books, 2007), p. 201.

2. Emily Sweeney, "Bill Belichick Starts Charitable Foundation," *Boston Globe*, August 16, 2014, https://www.bostonglobe.com/metro/regionals/south/2014/08/16/the-softer-gentler-side-bill-belichick/G8TJ1Jt3mGkNEAw9exiunN/story.html.

3. Price, p. 213.

4. "15 Legendary Bill Belichick Quotes About Tom Brady," Patriots.com, August 3, 2015, http://www.patriots.com/news/2015/08/03/15-legendary-bill-belichick-quotes-about-tom-brady.

CHAPTER 8: A TARNISHED LEGACY?

1. Michael Holley, *War Room* (New York: NY, HarperCollins, 2011), p. 131.

2. Ibid, p. 208.

3. Brian Burke, "Defending Belichick's Fourth-Down Decision," *New York Times*, November 16, 2009,

https://fifthdown.blogs.nytimes.com/2009/11/16/
defending-belichicks-fourth-down-decision/?_r=0.

4. Holley, p. 221.

5. Nick Underhill, "Bill Belichick on Ochocinco's Social Media Use: 'I Don't Twitter, I Don't MyFace, I Don't Yearbook,'" Mass Live, July 30, 2011, http://blog.masslive.com/patriots/2011/07/bill_belichick_on_ochocincos_s.html.

CHAPTER 9: ON TO CINCINNATI

1. Michael Holley, *Belichick and Brady* (New York, NY: Hachette Books, 2016), p. 289.

2. "Do Your Job: Bill Belichick and the 2014 Patriots," NFL Network special, September 9, 2015.

3. Kevin Van Valkenberg, ESPN, "How Malcolm Butler Made the Greatest Play in Super Bowl History," ESPN, December 8, 2015, http://www.espn.com/nfl/story/_/id/14286587/how-patriots-malcolm-butler-made-greatest-play-super-bowl-history-beat-seahawks.

CHAPTER 10: BELICHICK BURNISHES HIS CREDENTIALS

1. "15 Legendary Bill Belichick Quotes About Tom Brady," Patriots.com, August 3, 2015, http://www.patriots.com/news/2015/08/03/15-legendary-bill-belichick-quotes-about-tom-brady.

2. Tony Grossi, "Bill Parcells Speaks on Bill Belichick, Tom Brady, Evaluating QBS and More," ESPN.com, March 17, 2017, http://www.espn.com/blog/cleveland/post/_/id/3078/bill-parcells-speaks-on-bill-belichick-tom-brady-evaluating-quarterbacks-and-the-role-of-analytics-in-pro-football.

3. Robert Cocuzzo and Bruce A. Percelay, "Winning Combination," *N Magazine*, June 28, 2017, http://www.n-magazine.com/winning-combination/.

GLOSSARY

ACL Anterior cruciate ligament. When torn, this knee ligament requires a lengthy healing and recovery period.

blitz When a defense decides to send a player rushing after the quarterback rather than assigning him to stop the run or defend the pass.

bulletin board material Actions or statements that could be perceived as disrespectful of a team's opponent, potentially motivating them to play harder.

chop block A blocking technique, now illegal in the NFL, that involves an offensive player throwing himself at the legs of a defender, in order to knock him down.

clutch The ability to perform under pressure and make winning plays with a high degree of difficulty.

field goal An attempt to score three points by kicking the football between the goalposts.

film grinder Someone who studies football game film, drawing useful conclusions based on what he or she sees.

free agency The concept of players' eligibility, as free agents, to reach a contract agreement with any team they choose.

game plan The offensive and defensive strategies devised by a team in order to win a specific game.

Lombardi Trophy Named for former NFL coach Vince Lombardi, this trophy is awarded to the team that wins the annual Super Bowl.

playbook The collection of plays a team has practiced and may choose to run during a game.

pocket The space created for the quarterback by his offensive line, which blocks onrushing defenders.

practice squad The reserve players whose job it is to prepare starters to play another team by duplicating their style of play in practice.

presser Media slang for a press conference.

punt A kick that turns the football over to the other team, hopefully about forty yards from the line of scrimmage.

roster The list of players on a team and available to play in a game.

sack When a defender tackles a quarterback behind the line of scrimmage.

salary cap The limit the league puts on the amount of money that a team can spend on players' salaries.

scheme An offensive or defensive strategy developed by a team's coaching staff to coordinate players' efforts on the field.

scout A professional talent evaluator who watches athletes compete in order to determine if they would be a good fit for the scout's team.

zone coverage A defense in which players cover areas of the field rather than trailing offensive players.

FURTHER READING

BOOKS

Felger, Mike, with Ernie Palladino. *Tales from the New England Patriots Sideline: A Collection of the Greatest Patriots Stories Ever Told.* New York, NY: Skyhorse Publishing, 2017.

Frenz, Erik. *Bill Belichick vs. the NFL: The Case for the NFL's Greatest Coach.* Chicago, IL: Triumph Books, 2016.

Holley, Michael. *Belichick and Brady: Two Men, the Patriots, and How They Revolutionized Football.* New York, NY: Hachette Books, 2016.

Sports Illustrated Kids editors. *Big Book of Who: Football.* New York, NY: Time Inc. Books, 2015.

WEBSITES

The Bill Belichick Foundation

billbelichickfoundation.org

Make donations, seek financial assistance, or explore mentorship opportunities.

Patriots.com

www.patriots.com

Get an inside look at the New England Patriots, with interviews, news, game previews, and more.

FILMS

Do Your Job: Bill Belichick and the 2014 New England Patriots. NFL Network, 2015.

Do Your Job Part II: Bill Belichick and the 2016 New England Patriots. NFL Network, 2017.

A Football Life: Meet Bill Belichick. NFL Network, 2009.

INDEX

- - - - - - - - - - -